Losing My Breath

Losing My Breath

FROM LOSS TO TRANSFORMATION

Cindy Weaver

ISBN: 153503260X
ISBN 13: 9781535032605

Dedication

This book is dedicated to all broken-hearted warriors
Engage in your battle with courage
In the end, love wins.

Contents

Foreword

SOMETIMES WE MEET SOMEONE WHO changes our life for the better. That's what happened to me, three years ago, when I met Cindy Weaver.

Cindy walked into my office, wanting to connect with her daughter who had passed the year before, after being struck by a car driven by a young man who was texting. Immediately, her daughter Chloe made herself known to us. She sat on the couch behind Cindy and began to joke with her. I don't remember now what the exact words were, but I will never forget the feel of that session. The love and joy in the room was like nothing I had ever felt before. I knew instantly that sitting in front of me was a beautiful person and that my life would never be the same.

I became Cindy's therapist, yet time and time again, she was the one who taught me, through her dedication to healing, what the power of love, pain, skepticism, faith and deep inquiry can do to change our lives.

Every moment that Cindy and I have spent together has been filled with awe of the way Cindy walks and interacts with the world. She moves through her grief with grace and grit and has found a way to live, expand, and grow in the face of a profound trauma by staying deeply connected with whatever arises for her. She has allowed herself to have a new relationship with her daughter, with herself, and with the world around her.

In this powerful, vulnerable, and heart-opening book, Cindy shares with all of us her unique perspective, gift, and vision, and teaches us how to live inside the intimate dance between pain and joy, despair and hope, life and death. She offers us, when all seems lost, a way to grow amidst our grief, and reconnect again with ourselves. She shares her remarkable journey from inhabiting the story of death and returning to the story of life, and how in that transition, joy can return.

There are two other stories to tell when a loved one dies. The story of the physical, and the story of the spirit. Both are crucial, and necessary, and in *Losing My Breath,* Cindy has embraced and shared both. She encourages us to be open to, explore, and be unafraid of the emotions that occur when a loved one dies. To stretch our minds to the possibility of a different kind of relationship with that person, and even to thrive and dance while walking alongside the deepest pain.

For those who have experienced a similar loss, I hope the following pages bring you as much growth as they have me. I send my gratitude to Cindy and her family for showing not just me, but all of us, how to regain our essential breath during the deep and vulnerable pain that comes with a loss of this nature.

With profound and deep love,

~Cheryl Breault

Whole Body Wisdom
http://cherylbreault.com/

Author's Note

Over two years ago I showed up at the office of Cheryl Breault, for our regularly scheduled session, not knowing what to expect. Cheryl is a very gifted therapist, intuitive coach and energy practitioner. Our sessions ranged from grief work to spiritual direction to laughter. I had no agenda on that day but began telling her how my experience with losing Chloe made me feel like I was literally and metaphorically losing my breath. Shortly into our conversation, she looked up at me and said, "So you know you're going to write a book, right?" I said no, but deep inside I knew the answer was yes. A message came to Cheryl that Chloe would be helping me. Part of the content for the book came streaming out on that day, so fast I could barely keep up with the messages Cheryl was getting. The words I wrote on that legal pad were almost illegible as I worked to keep up with the stream of content that was coming through. I wrote horizontally and vertically, filling every space on the page. Random arrows were scattered in between thoughts trying to keep it all connected. I felt like we had both stepped into some kind of sacred space. When the session was done I folded that yellow paper into quarters and tucked it into my journal, not knowing what would become of it.

In later sessions I asked her why I would be writing a book. What purpose was there? Was it for me, for someone else? She said, "I really don't know," but she encouraged me to just ask the question.

Later that week I was driving up the canyon on my way home from work and I asked it again: "What purpose would there be for me in writing a book?" I had always thought that Chloe's role would be to provide content. This ended up being so far from the truth. The message in the canyon became clear, but it was not what I expected. The reason I am writing this book is for my own growth and healing; it is the journey, the process. Publishing the book holds its own purpose altogether, to give my story to another with the intention of helping or healing beyond myself. Chloe's role was actually different from what I had initially believed. It is her job to keep me focused on my own spirit and heart, to keep me from looking back into the physical loss and memory, and to help me see her in her own present spirit story, where she is now. This was necessary so that I would not become emotionally drained while writing. I could not, on any day, start writing without quieting my mind and asking for help. This kept me peaceful and on purpose.

One day, at the end of the third year, I started reflecting on what it was I had done to survive this unspeakable challenge. Everyone who experiences loss makes different choices and has different needs. I observed that there were four main streams that I had entered into; one was that of deep reflection: meditation, prayer, reading, and writing. One was working my life out at a physical and cellular level: dancing, energy medicine, horseback-riding, and yoga. Another was working with intuitive healers and mediums and learning my own way of communication with Chloe. The last was research: trying to figure out, at a more scientific level, what my brain was doing.

I considered organizing this journey chronologically by the last five years. But I realized that if you read "Year 3," there are places that still looked so much like "Year 1." I saw that in every year, I was learning something about each aspect of grief and growth and they were each creating a story of their own. Grief has had a type of evolution over time. For example, I felt myself moving from raw, sharp pain to an ache, to a soft sadness. This is a somewhat linear movement, however, my experience with loss and grief has not followed a formula and did not seem to progress through a series of stages. As soon as I would find myself in one stage, I would be back in an earlier stage, as if beginning again. I came to accept the randomness and just sat with each day as it came.

This book, primarily spanning the first five years after loss, is a progression from loss to transformation when you look at the entire experience. Each chapter begins with my thoughts, questions or discoveries, and several chapters are followed with journal entries from the five-year period. The journal entries are unedited in order to present my experience in its rawest, truest form. To summarize them would have removed the actual impact that I felt as I was moving through those days and moments.

The part of my experience that I became the most in awe of was the realization that an eternal connection was possible. Not only had I never experienced it, I had not heard others in my circles talk about it either. I didn't know where to file this experience. I had no background that told me how to navigate it or if I should even move in this direction. But as the dreams, messages and signs kept appearing, I realized they were keeping me connected to Chloe and moving me forward in my own life as well. I have included only a fraction of these experiences, to provide a window into how my connection with Chloe was possible. It is also my hope that others will realize how close their loved ones really are.

There was so much "boot camp" to go through to even bring myself to write this book. The biggest mountain was coming to terms with the fact that *this* was my story. I couldn't deny it, but I was hurt and angered by it. Why did I now have a story that Chloe was not a part of? My dream of watching my family grow and expand was lost, while I watched others get to enjoy the story that I wanted to live. As I wrote down my thoughts and experiences over the last five years, I never intended to write a book. It began as a necessary part of my survival. In time I was getting nudges from people, messages from Chloe and then some kind of internal prodding to do it, for whatever reason, I didn't know at the time. As I began moving through my story, more layers were being peeled back from my heart, at times bringing a release and at other times requiring a deeper dive into my pain.

As I wrote, I had to stay connected to my own heart and my own experience, even though I was sometimes tempted to try and figure out what others really wanted to hear. I had to stay true to myself to make sure I was telling my own story and not staging myself. I had to get out of my head, away from my fears and insecurities. Sometimes I began writing with my eyes closed, feeling my own experience and letting it pour onto the screen.

I spent the first months of this book-writing project trying to hide, even from myself. Trying to protect myself in case I failed. Somewhere along the way, I realized I was afraid to take the risk, to be vulnerable. What if I was just a crazy, grieving lunatic? But I decided to "jump," to tell my story, honestly and courageously. I shook off perfection and allowed my brokenness and my strength to flow out of my heart.

Thus, the journey of a lifetime began.

Prologue

It was a warm Sunday in October. My son, Dillon, aged 15, and I were at home when he asked if I would make a chocolate cake. Not too much on the agenda that day, so I ran to the grocery store. As I pulled back into my drive, a friend pulled in at the same time. She walked toward me, her face looking stricken, with no emotion. I was suddenly afraid that something might have happened to Herm as he was flying back from his golf event in Ohio. She began to speak:

"Chloe has been in a bike accident."
"What happened?"
"I don't know…She died."
"What?!"
"She was in a bike accident…and she died."

A lightning bolt ripped through me and froze my being. All I could do was call out Chloe's name. I ran into the house to find Dillon and just blurted it out. He cried; I held him. I went into a frenzy of making calls, trying to figure out how to tell Herm myself before he found out from someone else. When I called him to tell him to meet us in Boulder, he already knew. The minute his plane touched down, his phone began ringing.

I waited for him to come. I paced around and around the building where we had decided to meet, feeling nothing—not crying, just walking. His car pulled into the parking lot, I ran to him, we embraced and sobbed. I cried out Chloe's name over and over. We went down to a nearby river and sat on a bench. We clung to each other and cried. Dillon approached us, embraced Herm, and they both sobbed. We went to Greeley to tell our daughter, Hope, aged 22. My stomach ached, but I couldn't cry. I was frozen. We walked into her house, where she was sitting at the kitchen table. Herm walked over to her and immediately told her. She clung to him and just cried. "No, Chloe," she said repeatedly. I took her hand and brought her over to the couch and held her as she cried. I had no more tears, just ache and shock.

Then we all caught our breath and began talking.

That night and in the days ahead, I felt like I was walking in someone else's skin. Just a blur of plans and people and tattoos. On Tuesday, we went to Alamosa to gather Chloe's things. That was the hardest day yet. I walked around her room. A half-eaten burrito on a plate. Photos and junk creations. I went to her closet. I saw her sweatshirt. When I held it, I broke down and called out for her. My heart shattered as I repeated, "Chloe, where are you?" I lay on her bed, sobbing endlessly, with Herm and Hope around me. 20 years was not enough. The next days were filled with staring at walls, floors, and ceilings, surrounding each other when we collapsed, but not thinking much at all. Every breath was filled with the pain and emptiness of her absence.

The memorial service was surreal, like attending my daughter's graduation. We went out to visit the bike memorial at the scene of the accident. I walked up and down the grassy area, looking for any last trace of her. I lay on the ground and let the sun surround my body. It got quiet, and I heard the sound of a dove in the field. The quieter we became, the louder the dove sang.

On that day and all the days after, all I wanted was to go out into the woods and talk to Chloe. I became reclusive. I wouldn't go out of the house except to be in the woods. I slept as late as I could, got up for a few hours, and took long naps in the afternoon. Up for a few hours, and back to bed. Sleep was the only relief I could find. I became dreadfully afraid to be alone in the house. I sat on the couch and stared into my computer, doing anything that would distract me, unable to mobilize myself.

I didn't know what had happened, and yet, I did. Some part of me still believed that I would find her in the woods.

Introduction

Every great story is a love story.

—Deepak Chopra

I heard the creak of the 3-inch thick pine door as it swung back on its hinges, and footsteps came bounding across the hard-wood floor. "Hi, mommy, how are you?"

"I'm fine."

"Mom, what's wrong."

You could never fool Chloe, not as a child and not as teenager. It was somewhere in her junior year of high school when she asked that question. It had been a stressful day at work, but I didn't want to bother anyone or bring it into our family time. But Chloe could sense when words were not authentic, and so I proceeded to explain my day to her. She hopped up on the counter, sitting crisscross, spooning peanut butter straight out of the jar and into her mouth. This was a common after-school scenario.

Chloe was fiercely passionate about things she believed in. Yet in the midst of her passion, she was gentle and kind. She was funny. While on family trips, it was normal for her to break out into loud singing, often off-key, inviting us all to join in. If we travelled through a tunnel, she made sure everyone was holding their nose.

As a lover of animals, Chloe often begged to visit the humane society. I gravitated toward the cutest, gentlest animals, having disregard for felines and anything with a high squeaky "yip." But on one visit, as I was walking around, I found Chloe sitting beside an injured, tired dog. She didn't move from cage to cage but just sat with that dog, talking to it in soothing, comforting tones.

She scampered through the woods beside our house, collecting pine-cones, moss and mushrooms as big as a grapefruit. She thought she found an Indian burial ground once when she discovered some broken pottery buried in the earth (really they were just old dishes, but that was the nature of her imagination.)

Relationships were at the core of who she was. Chloe was a reader, a think-er, a seeker of the sacred. She did not need anyone or anything to motivate her; her motivation came from her own Spirit. She loved deeply and reveled in the presence of family and friends. She cared intensely about people in need. One Christmas when she was about 16 years old, all on her own, she gave each of us in the family t- shirts or hats that said "water" on them. Rather than buy other gifts for us, she had given her Christmas money to an organization that was drilling water wells in African communities that didn't have them.

She was a writer who recorded her thoughts and reflections on life. Some of these thoughts became songs. Her soothing voice filled our house as she played her guitar or her ten dollar piano.

She was earth and fire, wind and water.

I could never have imagined what a parent might go through when experienc-ing the loss of a child. I didn't want to know. But now, I knew. It started with a pattern of feeling split wide open, raw, bleeding, then became moments of nothing and yet constant pressure and pain. As a preacher's daughter, I grew up entrenched in the church and a multitude of ideas about who God was. Although my beliefs have always been fluid and changing as I experienced life, there has always been some semblance of "God" in my life. But now, what did I do with God? Nothing, really. I didn't know if he was there or if he wasn't. I had no idea how to approach a supreme being, nor did I understand what it meant to pray, or what the role of prayer was in my own grief. One thing I did know: he wasn't bringing her back.

During times of loss, I had always seen people running, falling into the arms of God. But that wasn't my experience. If God was supposed to be a parent type, a nurturing figure, protector, guardian, lover of my soul, then he had miserably failed me. Child of God? Any parent who would put a child through pain, who would stand by and watch the suffering, would be the one who had abandoned and neglected his or her own child. That is exactly how I felt: abandoned. I didn't know how to restore the trust I'd once had in this parent figure. I couldn't pretend. In my early visits to the woods, I could meditate, talk to Chloe, solicit the help of angels, guides, and guardians- my entire universal tribe, but the only thing I could say to God, as I had known him, was, "I'm here."

In the meantime, I became solely focused on my bleeding heart and on finding Chloe. I knew I would never find her as she had once been, that I could not touch or hold her, but I also knew that she had not left me. She had a deep connection with her family, and was strong-spirited and determined. She would find a way, and so would I. If all that is lost in death is physical form, then I knew we would be able to connect at a spirit level, but how that would happen, I didn't know at the time. Still, wherever she was now, I sensed that I could in some way connect with her.

I became an avid student of metaphysics and spiritual science, determined to learn what I could about the afterlife, what really happens, and who was out there to help me. I needed to know where Chloe was, and what our places were in relation to each other. I needed to know if our connection was eternal. I was open to any resolution I could find. If I came to a point where I couldn't find answers and had to accept the separation, then I would. But I would never needlessly break my connection and bond of love with her without a diligent search. Some people may resign themselves more easily to waiting until they die to be rejoined with their loved ones, but I wasn't going to wait that long if I didn't have to.

I read books voraciously—about angels, spirit helpers, afterlife, communication with loved ones—trying to learn more and, at times, trying to find inconsistencies in their messages so I could just return to my previous belief system without this challenge. But a deepening of my spirit was taking place as I continued this journey. I was being taken to a new level of spiritual understanding and experience than I had ever known.

I began to increase my times of meditation and sitting in the silence of the woods, expanding every sense within me. I closed my eyes and practiced listening deeply, from the call of a bird to the subtle flutter of the Aspen leaves. I gazed at the shape of the stones at my feet and the asymmetrical shapes of the trees. I felt the ground beneath me, became conscious of the sun's warmth, the wisp of hair blowing against my cheek and every sensation within my body. What happened in the days and months to follow was nothing short of miraculous. I learned how to interpret Chloe's messages. I could ask for what I needed and, as I sharpened my senses and learned her language, I could begin to hear and see her. I started to recognize and separate when I was experiencing trauma and when I was experiencing loss. Although they weave in and out of each other like a tapestry, I saw that, at times, I was just merely collapsing, as if my body was trying to release its deep shock. Other times, I felt a deep ache for her to be with me, to see her, to talk to her; I felt the overwhelming loss of her. Gradually, I began to see the larger scope of life and death (although I wasn't happy with the set-up); I could acknowledge that I didn't understand my loss or the plan for life and death, but I could start trusting that there was a divine purpose in it all.

My therapists and spiritual guides kept me healthy and whole. I valued them for helping me to deepen my experience while staying grounded in my life here and for keeping me in check, making sure I was living my reality and not pretending.

I had always heard murmurings about contacting loved ones, but had never needed to know the truth about it. For the most part, I thought psychics and mediums were entertainers and, in some cases, associated with "the dark side" or "playing with the devil," both phrases I had heard growing up. I have found none of these misconceptions to be true. My experience with mediums, spiritual guides, and intuitive healers has led me to some deeply spiritual experiences.

In addition to seeking this eternal connection on the spiritual plane, I attempted to point myself in a healing direction on the physical plane. I found this happening by attending to my passions, nurturing old ones and pursuing new ones. I returned to dance, spent more time in the woods, took my first yoga class, began equine therapy and bought a Native American flute. My need for writing became a daily practice, although it often held more pain than pleasure. You would think that all this grief work would help to ease the pain and slow the tears, but in truth this was the work that helped me cry and walk through the center of my pain. In between tears, life began expanding to a deeper, richer place, while allowing pain to exist alongside it. My heart ached so often, but I didn't feel despair or hopelessness. I found myself no longer just waiting to get to the end of my life so I could have rest and see Chloe. I began walking beside her in the very present moment.

CHAPTER 1

Grief

"If you bring forth that which is within you, then that which is within
you will be your salvation. If you do not bring forth that which
is within you, then that which is within you will destroy you".

—FROM THE GNOSTIC GOSPELS

TELLING "ABOUT" MY EXPERIENCE IS not the same as "feeling" it which is the
reason I have chosen to use many of my journal entries. To merely summarize this type of experience does not offer an adequate picture unless it is, on
some level, felt. However, to give my intimate experience is also an exercise in
vulnerability, a scary one. And yet, if I choose not to reveal myself to others, I
remain protected, which only perpetuates more hiding and my authentic self
dies. It is my hope that, as I offer my experience here, others will honor their
own journey as well, staying true to the timeline of grief and all of its paths.

In the first months after losing Chloe, I experienced a great deal of anxiety and fear. The fear was based in the irrational idea that this event of loss
was going to repeat itself. My body was trying to release the shock, something
humans don't do well. I didn't feel like this was a time to be a hero and allowed myself to take anxiety meds, but as sparingly as I could. They helped
to ease my body so that I wouldn't be presented with an additional challenge.
In time, I started observing why I was having anxiety and when it was happening. I saw that anxiety was really just created by whatever it was that I was

holding and not releasing. When I embraced my tears and cried as deeply as I needed to, it relieved the anxiety because it was bringing up my soul contents and releasing them. The other "fix" for my occasional fear and anxiety was lying directly on the earth and breathing. In time, both of these practices began to replace the meds.

My journal entries reflect that grief was new to me. It was an experience and an exploration all at the same time. Moving through grief required me to lay out my thoughts and emotions on the pages of my journal in the rawest form, and—because of the random nature of grief—I found myself cycling through periods of light and dark in patterns that endured for the next two years. It also demonstrates how broadly grief affected every aspect of my being, from the inability to focus, fatigue, social awkwardness to my entire world view.

As I prepared to write the section on Grief, I poured over my journal entries, almost as an onlooker. Feeling a sadness for what was lost, contemplating my own heartbreak in those beginning days and years. I sift through my words trying to decide what is important to share and what should be left out, if anything. Do I give my heart to the world? Would it be better to just provide a summary of my experience with grief and move on? I know the answer is "no." I am trying to escape the vulnerability it will take to bare my soul with all of its pain and ugliness. How can we walk honestly through life with each other if we continually hide? I can only honor myself and my readers by offering my experience as it truly happened.

LOSING MY BREATH

I cried in sounds I have never heard. Sometimes I almost stopped breathing, and I had to stop and take a breath. I am carrying her sweatshirt with me everywhere, like a child who has to have her blanket. I feel desperate to have her back, but I can't.

I sat down on the couch, I closed my eyes and just started breathing. Every breath contained pain and loss. I wanted to hear Chloe's footsteps, her voice, her laughter, feel her hug. I just said what I was feeling: that I felt so sad without her, I didn't know how to make it to the end of this life. Then the tears came. After that, I just sat and talked to her.

SEASONS OF GRIEF

I find no difference in grief and death. In death, there is grief, but grief itself is death. It is not a mere missing what has been lost, the absence of a physical presence, but a personal death ensues. The process becomes one of trying to find yourself again and grieving the absence of the child at the same time. You lose what you have loved, and you lose yourself. It all comes crashing down to nothing before it can be rebuilt. It is the loss of dreams. New dreams will have to come, but not now.

You just can't get around it, no matter how hard you try to push it away or yell or scream or ignore it, or sing or dance. The grief will just wait for you until you acknowledge that it hurts and release it. I'm starting to see a cycle in the process of grief. I feel depressed or just detached, no highs or lows, just existing. I don't like that feeling. It's like I'm not even alive. Then I just break down. I feel like my heart is going to fall out of my body. I've never cried like that before. It is such a new experience. Then, after I cry, there is a calm, and all of a sudden I am feeling life again, even if it is painful. I prefer feeling pain to feeling nothing at all.

TEARS

When I woke up this morning, I didn't want to get out of bed. I went downstairs. Herm made me some tea. I talked with Hope. I knew she had been in the living room watching TV. She said every time she closed her eyes, she thought of Chloe, and she couldn't sleep. I had such a heaviness descend on me. Just the thought of getting through the day seems overwhelming. I went upstairs to read. I couldn't focus or comprehend anything. I just sat on my bed with my head against the wall and put my hand on my heart as if to keep it from falling out. My whole body just breathed pain in and out.

Later I went back downstairs to try again. It is Sunday, at two thirty, the day of the week and the time that Chloe left us on October 24. The shock is lessening, although the disbelief is ever-present. The sharp, unrelenting pain comes in waves rather than feeling so permanent. The fear and anxiety is lessening. I feel myself dropping into a pattern of two or three days of calm and then one or two days of storms. Yesterday, I wanted to clean out some drawers and closets, but everywhere I went, Chloe was there. I couldn't even discard old medical statements. I went to my closet. I found a big card that she had made that said, "I Love You Mom." It felt as if the entire house was breathing with Chloe's presence, only it was painful, not comforting. I counted the hours until bedtime. I did the dishes, the laundry, and some cleaning. I felt a numb sadness all day. Later, I spent some time in quiet meditation, talking to Chloe, sharing my love with her.

The thing about this grief and loss process is that sometimes, the sorrow permeates your entire being, physically, spiritually, and emotionally. It is just unspeakable and unbearable. Other times, there is inspiration from Chloe's life and death. And then there is also a feeling of my soul deepening. I have always heard about living in each moment, being conscious of it and just being right there in whatever presents itself. Then there are the moments when everything just feels like a tangled mess. But that is not what I'm feeling tonight, and I am grateful.

Yesterday morning when I woke up, I felt shaky, with a sense of fear. I went on with my day. Later, Herm told me my whole body had been shaking in the night. He tried to put his hand on my leg to calm me, but I just kept shaking. When animals are afraid or in trauma, their bodies shake, and then they release the shock and resume their activities. Humans don't operate that instinctually. We tend to hold instead of release. I had really not cried for several days, just a flat existence where sorrow and laughter were able to coexist. All of a sudden, I began to cry, at first a few tears, and then it plunged to the depth of my soul and it moved from crying to weeping. Every breath was audible, and I could only utter Chloe's name.

SHOCK

People ask me how I am and I am honest, but I mostly speak in general terms, except to a few. The real truth that has been gripping me is the thoughts that keep playing in my mind: "Chloe can't be gone. I have to find a way to get her back. Either she has to come to me, or I have to go to her . . ." I can't tell people this, because it is a totally irrational thought and, at the same time, a real one to me. I have lost any acceptance of her being gone. I don't want to work on moving forward. I just want to sit with her and be with her. I will have years to move forward and miss her. If I could, I would disappear for a while just to be with her. I don't care about anything else around me. I can't find meaning anywhere. I always knew that people die. I saw it every day. I knew it was a part of life. But now, I realize that I didn't know what death was at all. I feel confused and disoriented. And yet, I can sit at a basketball game and socialize and even laugh. I am two people.

POSSESSIONS

Chloe's piano has been sitting outside our house with a tarp over it. I recall her excitement at finding this ten-dollar piano and how impossible it seemed to actually get it into the house. But with some help, we did it. Herm got a call today that someone would be coming to get it, a decision we had reluctantly made. He got off the phone and cried. I think we will leave when they come to take it away. We could have kept it, but there are possessions that hold you captive to your grief and slow the process of healing.

This week, I was able to put Chloe's picture up. I put one in my bedroom and one in the kitchen. I have not been able to have her pictures up before because it just reminded me that she wasn't here. I can look at the picture CDs that her friends have made. Even though there are still times of collapse and deep crying, the times in between seem to offer more peace.

I often catch myself with thoughts like, "I want to tell Chloe that," or, "I need to make that appointment for Chloe," and then I remember that she's not here. Yesterday, I was going to clean out my files. When I looked at my document folder, I momentarily thought, "I should probably keep Chloe's papers," but then I caught myself. I still have that feeling that I should keep them. But for what? In the event that she comes back? Those are times that the reality hits like a hard slap in the face with the sting that follows.

ONLY FUNCTIONAL

I am glad I am able to go back to work and function decently, but it is difficult to do anything other than my primary responsibilities, answering e-mails, paperwork, and so on. It seems like grieving becomes a preoccupation. My mind is working hard to make sense of it, to sort it out, adjust to the change, reworking my life view, crying, getting myself to move through the day. Today, household tasks seem daunting. I just want to lie on the couch and stare into space. The extent of the loss seems to become larger each day, even though I can function, laugh, and smile. I just can't see where my place in the world is anymore. I thought I had some kind of sense of that before. I don't know how to move through life when I have no understanding of it. Sometimes I feel like a robot. I do my job, attend events, and finish tasks. My entire life is really about this journey with and without Chloe.

Sometimes I feel good and then, all of a sudden, I feel so far away. I thought death was just about missing someone. But it is so much more. It is the loss of yourself and your identity. I poured myself into Chloe, and then she was just gone. I don't know how to interpret my world or my life. I take on my responsibilities, but inside I feel like a nomad, a wandering soul. I can't find my tears, and I need them. My stomach has been distressed for the past few days. I feel I am holding too much in. I eat, feel sick, don't eat, and get hungry. I am mostly drinking water.

My courage has collapsed into tears and grief rushes in like a tsunami.

SOCIAL AWKWARDNESS

I went to Dillon's basketball game yesterday. It was a summer tournament, so I didn't know any of the parents. I was sitting there, and three women were sitting on the bench below me. I heard them introducing themselves to each other, asking about how many children they each had, and talking about them. I froze. I hadn't been in that situation, and I was afraid I would be the next one they asked. What was I supposed to say? If I told the truth, I would stop the conversation, rain on their social parade. If I answered in a more acceptable way, then I wouldn't be true to myself or my experience.

I am invited to parties, women's groups, lunches and numerous other social events, but I am terrified of them. While they should offer distraction, friendship and support, I am afraid of the conversation, like I am developing social skills all over again. What do I talk about? The weather? How the "kids" are? Work? It all seems so pointless and painful. What if someone I don't know asks me how many kids I have? What do I do with that?

I repeatedly drive to these social events, pull into a parking space, turn my car off and sit there. In a matter of minutes, I start the car and drive home. It is impossible for me to face this now foreign territory.

The phone rings, but I cannot answer it. I don't know what or who will be on the other end. I haven't answered the phone for a year and a half. I just listen to the messages. I don't answer my cell phone unless I'm sure I know who is calling. I have wondered if I'll ever answer the phone again. But tonight I read a story about a man who didn't answer the phone for four years after his father died. Now I feel like I am OK. I can just relax and know that this is a long journey, no matter what anyone looking in may think.

We no longer have a landline.

SATURDAY SADNESS

One of the things I read is that if you present yourself to others as being all right, they will be comforted, but you will turn to stone. What you experience must be felt and acknowledged, honestly.

I lay on the floor to do my yoga. My stomach was unhappy, and I just needed to lie there. I did figure eights across my body and listened to my binaural track. Then I lay my hand on my stomach and said, "It's OK, you don't have to hold it, you can let go." Then I started to cry. I felt such a deep loss. Every time I stopped, I would start again. After a while, Oscar, Chloe's dog, came over and put his paw on my heart and then laid his head on me. I held him by my side, and we just lay there for some time, going in and out of tears.

In the evening, I was edgy. By bedtime, I felt better, but cried some. I woke up at 2:30 a.m., feeling distraught. I thought about all the years it would be that I would have to live without Chloe and even more years that Hope and Dillon would live without her. In that moment, I wanted to die. I fell asleep, and I was all right this morning. In fact, I felt an overwhelming sense of "something" all around me. Messages came at me, and it was like I felt a vibration in my soul. I had entered into some kind of divine, sacred space.

TSUNAMI DAYS

Life seems so backward. I thought this would be a progression of time that would get better with each day. Last year when I returned to work, I was running on some kind of adrenaline, even though there were tears every weekend. Now, I am crawling through each day, hoping to make it to the end. I sleep at every opportunity to escape the reality that still exists. I thought maybe it would have receded by now, but I feel like I get a hard slap in the face every morning. I want to break glass, throw rocks. I feel like a failure, even though that is so irrational. I couldn't make life work out. It just all went crazy. In this entire year, I have never been worried about myself. But now I feel so unraveled, I wonder if I will ever recognize myself again. The only consolation is that I know I have been here before, and in time, it will pass.

TEARS AND PEACE

I went outside on the porch to do my yoga. I figured I might just need some physical exercise. I am getting to where I can go through the first poses in a total state of meditation. But when I began the first one, I just started sobbing. I wanted Chloe to come back so badly. My daughter was born, and then she died. It is still so disorientating and shocking. It just kept on. I was shaking. I moved to the next pose, but it continued. I knew I just had to let it be, no matter how long it took, and in time, it subsided. I kept breathing, meditating, and moving. Then some peace started replacing the sorrow. I was feeling calm, and I talked to Chloe and moved into gratefulness. Now I feel OK. I don't feel like I'm trying to fight through my day. I just needed to let my sorrow take its place. I had a pretty good day. There was light.

Coming to the end of the summer, I have a deep sadness, like Chloe never came home from summer camp. I remember how happy I was just to see the kids after they had been gone for a week. I've had a deep ache inside me, knowing how real this is. I've figured out that it's not really a matter of waiting until it goes away. It will most likely just be there for me to work with throughout life. So I guess what I'm feeling is despondent and yet living. I don't worry too much about happiness. Some days I feel it, but if I don't, I just let it be.

I'm not sure how I am, really. I can't seem to resolve myself. Who am I? How am I? What am I? I am this person who is engaged in living, who is good and happy. I am this person who is broken, crying, screaming, silent, invisible, not wanting to be seen. I can't answer the question, "How are you?" But I always say, "Good," because that is the truth and it is also a lie. I am functioning, I even have moments of happiness and I am seeing beauty again. But I am, at the same time, distraught at moving through my days without Chloe.

Life and death are struggling with each other again. Sometimes they hold hands and sometimes they push and shove. I am not one or the other; I am both. Like a centaur who is half-man, half-animal. But they know how to live together; they are comfortable with their identity. I am a stranger to this new identity. Living with pain, not chasing it away. It's a new book, and I feel like a new character, having difficulty remembering much about the old character. Who was I? How did I feel? What did I think? Who will I be next?

ONE-YEAR ANNIVERSARY

I don't know what this day has been, really. I feel quiet, but not emotional. Maybe a little far away. I'm not reliving the events of October 24, 2010. I've had some times of remembering what happened, but then I've just said, "But that was last year." I actually experienced more anxiety and tears in September with the anticipation of what the anniversary would bring. The feeling that it was going to happen again, and not knowing what I was supposed to do to mark it, or did I need or even want to. Cards came, which brought mixed emotions. I wanted them to stop coming so that I wouldn't have to be reminded of the raw feelings of those first days. At the same time, I felt honored that people remembered and cared.

We had decided to fly to OH for a Cleveland Browns football game. I woke up early in the morning, lying in the still twilight of the sun beginning to peek in the window of our hotel room. I breathed the words, "This is the day my daughter died." I was not emotional, but almost just observant. I had more of a feeling of her quiet transition from one world to the next.

Today, I feel like I just want her back.

Unchosen Broken Heart

She was born, I loved her, was in love with her small life. She grew, we grew. She left. I am heartbroken with no hope of bringing her back or ever having her in my physical life again. I loved her so much. I wanted her in my life forever. I can't have her.

I am bleeding, falling weak into myself. Twenty years of a living, breathing life flow out of me, leaving me breathless. I can't stop it; no one can. It is a passage I must go through, almost a ritualistic death. Then, and only then, will I start feeling the movements of life.

Heartbreak is something I understand and wish I didn't. It rapes the depth of your soul and leaves you empty. It robs you of your dreams and purpose and leaves you surviving each minute. It makes you fight for your life, and yes, you may grow and become better, but still, part of your heart has been cut out and it will never be returned. It pushes you into the shadows while you work every minute to come into the light. And no one will know because you don't want to be a burden, you want to be a success story, a survivor. I cry, I weep, I ache, but I live.

The Last Good-Bye

I looked to my left and saw the Fairgrounds. The words came out of my mouth as a single breath. "This is the last place I saw Chloe, the last time we hugged, the last time we said, 'I love you.'" It was La Junta, CO, the last Mennonite Relief Sale I ever went to, and the last place I would see Chloe. I'll always remember that day like a poem.

Hope and Dillon had come with us, and Chloe drove up to meet us. We checked into our hotel. In the middle of the night, the droning whistle of a train sounded outside the window. Chloe woke Dillon up to listen to it.

The next day, the girls got up early to run the 5K. Chloe had left her sweat-shirt somewhere on the course and went to look for it. As we saw her coming around the corner in the distance, we all hid behind a car and jumped out at her when she got close. After that, we wove our way through the craft building, touching and examining unique creations, laughing and greeting people, eating homemade pastries and apple cider.

Then Chloe said, "Mommy, come shop with me." We went together, and she found this crazy hat. I bought it for her, and she loved it.

Then we went to buy Carrie some bread. She wanted to get her something because she had often let Chloe stay with her.

"Mommy, what do you think I should get for her?" I picked up a loaf of bread with a red ribbon.

When it was time to part, she began hugging each of us good-bye. I was on the other side of our vehicle. She came around and hugged me. I said, "I love you, Chloe." She said, "I love you, too, Mommy."

I was not looking forward to this return trip. I had an almost sick feeling, but I thought it would be helpful for me to be back in the place where I had last said good-bye to Chloe. I thought I was all right. I was driving through town to the place where we were to meet Herm and Hope was talking beside me, and then it just poured out. I tried to hold it back, but I couldn't. We pulled into the parking place and Hope suddenly realized I was crying. She asked me what was wrong, but I couldn't get out any words. She jumped out of the car and came over and opened my door and just held me. I couldn't talk. I just kept crying. Then finally, I was able to say, "It's this place."

She said, "I know."

My heart does not know how to hold this last good-bye. Sometimes with grate-fulness, sometimes in shattered pieces.

SUNDAY FLASHBACKS

I took Dillon to Boulder. On the way home, I looked at the clock. It was around the time that I found out about Chloe on a Sunday. I started crying again. The whole thing started playing over in my mind. Then I drove up the drive, and I remembered it all just like it was happening today. I went into the house. I started to cook, but then I became overwhelmed. I put my head into my coat and sobbed uncontrollably. Herm came up and held me. I was trying to tell him how it all happened, how I found out on a Sunday when he was gone. He couldn't understand me through my tears. Hope came up and held me. I told them why I was so affected. Later, Herm said, "Now I understand why Sundays are so hard for you. I'll try not to schedule work on Sundays."

I've realized that Sundays are the most difficult days for me, and they often carry over into Monday. Today is especially difficult; no coasting through this day. It is a sunny October day. Dillon and I are here, Herm is gone. I was planning on getting groceries but felt slightly petrified of creating the same scenario. It feels a little more like trying to live through the shock and trauma again. I have shattered once already. The waves of aftershock ripple through my body. There is a feeling of impending doom. The day Chloe died, I didn't know it would happen. Today I feel like I already know it's going to happen, even though this is not rational. She's not going to die today; she already has. I don't know if my body knows this yet. It is still in high gear on days like this, trying to work it out.

LEAVING FIFTY SUNDANCE CIRCLE

We made a decision to leave our log home on Sundance Circle. It was somewhat like letting the piano go. Wanting to hold on, but feeling captive to it at the same time. The joy, the light and the happiness once felt there was clouded by the vacancy Chloe's absence left. Every day when I returned from work and opened that thick solid wood door, it descended on me. Her room holds sweet memories, but the memories only remind me of what no longer exists, that I don't see her movements, hear her voice or her song. There is darkness here that may get better with time or it may consume me.

We didn't have far to move, just on the other side of town, to a beautiful, healing ranch. I could already feel a lighter energy in the new house and the land, but I had to close the chapter on Sundance Circle. I wanted to continue living at Sundance, but I knew I needed to go, to look ahead.

After most of our possessions had been moved to the new house, I went back to the old house. I knew I needed to do that one more time. I walked into the emptiness. I looked up into the ceiling at the rich, warm logs. A dream, a family. I can't seem to let go of the memories of moving in. The excitement, the laughter, the new start, and all the beauty of the woods at our front door. Now, it held me captive to the past; it held pain. I just stood there, feeling nothing and everything. I went into Chloe's room. I talked to her about the hard times and the good times. I sat down and leaned my head against the wall. I cried. God, please get me to the end of this life.

I went downstairs and finished packing up the back room. I left. I feel more lost than found.

LIFE MOVIES

After six weeks of not feeling much of anything, trying to get through the holidays and the move, not wanting to feel pain, tired of sadness, everything started to come to the surface again.

Friday, I left school and started driving home. The first week after Chloe's death started playing over and over again in my head, like a movie that kept rewinding. The terrifying shock, the accident, being handed her phone and her ring, the site where she died, cleaning out her room, crying, excruciating pain that wouldn't let go, but just pressed into my heart. I started to cry. I didn't want that to be part of my life story. I started thinking about how our lives are made up of different movies. Some are dramatic, some are filled with love; some are exciting, some challenging. But I have a horror movie in my collection now. Finding out that Chloe died was horrific. Living without her is terrifying, disorienting, and heartbreaking. Now I am in the process of creating my next movie. What will it be? What will I create? I won't have control over everything. Can I make it one of the better movies I have had, even without Chloe?

GRIEF: IT ISN'T ALWAYS WHAT IT IS

We headed toward our destination: Mount Princeton Hot Springs. The sun was shining, and I was looking forward to the days ahead, not anticipating *how the location would affect me. As we passed through Leadville, it all came rushing back, like being sucked through an inescapable tube into the past. It was the same route we had taken to Alamosa and it was suddenly Tuesday, October 26, 2010, not Friday, 2015, and we were headed to pick up Chloe's belongings. I saw the sign: "Burrito, Burrito, Burrito." It was a sharp remembrance:*

Traveling down to pick up Chloe's belongings, I saw the sign and laughed. In the same moment, wondering why I laughed, what it meant to laugh, how I could even laugh. It was as though I was grasping for some normal, a diversion from the inevitable.

The images started playing like a bad movie. The first, frozen step into her room. All of her quirky creations, her keys, the cough medicine reminding me of our phone conversation that week:

"Mom, what should I take for my cold?"

"Chloe, I wish I could take care of you."

"I do too, Mom."

A sick, tight feeling gripped my stomach without letting go. Her bed was made, things in order. It was her; every piece breathed Chloe. I opened the closet and saw her green Nederland sweatshirt that we had given her. The first really soul-splitting, ripping, heart-crushing pain engulfed me. I got up and grabbed a bag, fiercely stuffing the things in, not stopping to let them elicit any emotion. I stuffed and packed in a frenzy. Her bike helmet. A sweeping question: was she wearing it? Probably not, or it wouldn't be here. But it wouldn't have protected her anyway. Herm carried the boxes and bags as fast as I could pack. Then we sat and had soup and bread with her house-mates as if Chloe had never left; it was just a meal, and they told us they had given Chloe the job of "caretaker of all living things." The memory of that day still holds the same emotional charge.

We arrived at Mount Princeton at night, and it was dark. We had a relaxing meal, a drink, and a movie. I forgot about the sign and the stirring in my heart and stomach.

The next day held glorious sunshine and relaxation. As we drove into town to eat, I observed that the land was beautifully and painfully almost identical to Alamosa, the place where Chloe lived and died. I had not yet made any comments to Herm about my experience. I said nothing, just feeling a deep, volcanic trembling. We ate, soaked in the hot springs and were happy. It went on like this. There were painful moments from breathing in this land and its memories, but they were generally replaced by happy times. I never talked about what I felt.

On the last night, we enjoyed food and music and conversation. When we finished, we drove down to the river. Herm brought the car up to the edge of a cliff with a swift-flowing river below. In reality, he hadn't really brought it that close. I don't like cliffs, but I'm not terrified of them. Then, a sudden rush of terror came over me, and I shouted, "Stop!" I said it three times. I opened the door and turned to an open meadow, heading the opposite direction. I wanted to run and run and not stop.

We went back to the lodge in silence. I was too shaken to speak. When we pulled into our parking spot, I asked, "Why didn't you stop?"

He said, "I'm sorry, I really didn't know you felt that way. And I did stop. I wasn't really that close." I broke, I sobbed. I asked him to leave me alone for a while. Everything came pouring out like a frozen snow mass that suddenly melts and has nowhere to go, but can only make a mad, rushing exit. And then I knew. It became so clear. It wasn't about the cliff; it was about this place I kept going to in silence, this barren absence and excruciating remembrance. So I turned my heart to face Chloe, not the cliff, and I expressed everything that had been wanting to come out. In the end, I asked Chloe to show me the beauty of this place.

I returned to the room, emotionally spent, but peaceful. I explained to Herm that the subtle fear of being too close to the edge was really only a trigger for all that I had been ignoring and holding in over the last few days, I just hadn't recognized how deeply it was affecting me. He said he understood. Because his work had brought him to this area and to Alamosa several times, he had had more opportunities to work through it. He thanked me and said it made sense now.

Look carefully, look deeply. When you think you are experiencing one thing, in truth, it may be something quite different that is actually looking for an open door, a way out. All I had experienced and not acknowledged that week found its way out when we drove up to the cliff. One quick gasp of being too close to the edge brought all of my painful emotions tumbling out.

CREATING WARRIORS

I move through the world as a warrior now—stronger and more courageous than I ever knew possible, but also deeply wounded. Sometimes, I stop and address my wounds. Other times, I have to keep moving or I know I will die. A warrior has to be strong, courageous and brave in the face of deep challenge. A warrior does not know how it's going to play out, but pushes forward in the face of uncertainty. The warrior hurts, but continues to fight in order to get to a better place. The alternative to not being a warrior is to be consumed by the challenge.

Today I received a picture from my daughter, Hope, taking a bath in the river, pouring water over her head. As the frigid water splashed over hair, her head was thrown back, her face shining with exuberant joy. One can only understand the depth of this joy by seeing the journey that she has faced, the rugged terrain traversed.

Four years ago, she lost her sister, Chloe—her best friend. On one particular morning, I heard a faint sobbing from a corner of the house. I followed it to Chloe's closet, where she lay in a collapsed heap. My maternal instincts were triggered. I had to fix this, that's my job. My mind raced, trying to find the healing balm, the pain reliever or even the promise that it would be over soon, that life would return to the safe, secure landscape we had known. But my hands were empty, I had nothing to offer her in this broken state.

I got down on my hands and knees and crawled into that closet. I laid behind her, wrapping her up and crying with her. Our bodies trembled together. They relaxed. We breathed and cried again, until the pain crashed over us and we were washed up on the shore of that closet floor.

One of the greatest challenges for me in losing my 20-year-old daughter was also losing my role as healer, fixer, and savior for my other two children, Dillon and Hope. I vacillated between anger—that they had to endure such a challenge at their young ages, and sadness—that the world had now become an unsafe place. The magical fairytale world I wanted to create for them had all but crumbled.

I realized that I had not prepared my children to become warriors in the world, but instead I was rushing in to manage their environment, to keep them pain-free instead of letting them squirm and squiggle and fight to develop the strength they needed for life.

As the days progressed, I began to see a surprising evolution happen. While I could be with them and there for them, this was now a path they were going to have to walk together and alone. They collapsed, they got up. They cried and laughed. They stepped out. I was there, beside them, but they were choosing the warrior path by themselves. I watched Dillon develop a deeper compassion for people. Hope chose new practices of yoga, writing, art, and meditation.

My children have taught me to step back, to be okay with pain and struggle. The result is not enduring hardship, but a blossoming courage and fierce determination to stay alive. Not only do they move through the world as warriors now, but they stop to heal the wounded.

A NEW TIME

Life just feels so crazy. I can feel good and then crash so hard in a matter of seconds. There is no changing it. I am more silent now, more heartbroken, and yet, somehow, I am able to live. Talking about it doesn't change it. Everyone wants me to feel better. No one wants me to hurt. Most people care about my loss but, they are through the shock of it and not really grieving anymore. I have no resentment or judgment for anyone's reaction to me. I feel cared for. I just can't be honest and I don't know how to pretend, so the tragedy piece of my life will be mine now, and I will continue to journey through it. I have moved into this time where I don't talk about it much. But there is so much still inside me, this wounded part of me that I live with. Sometimes I want to scream at everyone, wanting them to feel it too, but I don't. I do what I know I need to do to move through life. I let myself feel it. I honor it and don't push it away. I bleed. I don't feel bad that I am no longer wearing it all on my sleeve.

    I want people to be able to get on with their lives. But I can only live my own timeline. I would rather have the peace and freedom to do and feel what I need to. I know what is inside me. I didn't ask for this challenge, but it is here, and so I will live it out, in my own time. I know that I will never be the same person I was. I have lost myself, I have died. I am trying to create a new and better person, but it takes so much work and energy to find myself. I can't yet feel like I used to. My mental processing is diminished. I have to concentrate harder with everything I do. I don't want anyone to fix me so they can feel better, but I so desperately want to become reclusive again. At times, I feel like a lone wolf, traveling the landscape solo, and yet deeply connected. I move through life differently, carrying, cradling this fragile, tender package.

    I feel like I am trying to make a transition from acute or short-term grief to long-term grief, and I find myself struggling to find my place again. I think the difference is that with initial grief, people gather tightly around you, they walk closely with you. In the beginning, life doesn't have much normalcy; the loss is out in front, the entire landscape of life. Long-term grief is a regaining of some normalcy to life and living. A time of letting go of that tight circle that is carrying you and continuing a more solo journey, although not totally alone. I need a sense of normal in my life. I don't want to be the oddball grieving woman. I don't want my whole identity to be my loss. I want people to see me for who I am first and my pain second. Plus, it is too much to ask of those in my life to still carry my pain. The difficult thing that comes with this is that I feel like it will be forgotten, I will be forgotten, Chloe will be forgotten.

    I know I still have work to do. I fall to pieces, I am shattered. There is never a day I don't feel it. The shock and feeling have left to a degree, but still exist. I cry, I become despondent and detached, staring at ceilings, walls, and floors. I lose my appetite, become irritable, and want to disappear. I constantly work on regaining trust and confidence in life. I have bouts of anxiety and fear. I often don't want to be close to anyone, as there is the lingering reality of losing them. I protect my heart. Life is work with moments of joy. I am working to allow myself to be happy, to figure out what happiness means now and how to obtain it. I think I am functioning well and surviving, but I have realized that real happiness, or its new definition has become elusive. Life will not return in the absence of pain, but in the midst of it. Chloe's death, as her entrance into life, has left me with scars. Scars do not disappear, but you live with them.

"Real grief is not healed by time . . . if time does anything, it deepens our grief. The longer we live, the more fully we become aware of who she was. Love often makes itself visible in pain."

—Henri Nouwen

CHAPTER 2

A Place Between
Three Trees

I BEGAN GOING TO THE woods several weeks after Chloe died. I would lay on the earth and sometimes weep and other times feel energy and healing being drawn into my body. I began talking to her. In one of the first conversations, I said, "So, *what*—it's just over? After nurturing and growing the deepest of connections, it's just done?"

I knew that Chloe was physically gone, but I didn't believe for one minute that the connection of our spirits and hearts was done. The answer I had always heard for dealing with death was, "she is happy and you'll get to see her again when you die." There was no way I was waiting that long! And yet, I knew that maybe it wasn't up to me. Still, I was unable and unwilling to accept the only answer that had ever been offered to me, to wait.

I asked Chloe if it was over. I heard her say immediately, "Our relationship is not over, but the language will change." I didn't know what she meant, but I knew at that point that she was right there. I could pursue my quest to find her and understand what life and death really are. I began to study, meditate, pray, and feel. Shortly after the message from Chloe, I was reading a book, and it mentioned the same idea—that it was possible to continue contact, but you had to learn the language of your loved one.

And so I gave myself to silence, listening, feeling, and being. My senses began to grow and become finely tuned. I was finding that I could now ask Chloe questions and receive answers. She began showing up in my life.

Going to that place in the woods was necessary to nurture that connection. It allowed me to cry, be at total peace, communicate with Chloe, and just sit in silence with her.

The following journal entries span the first two years. They are recorded here in unedited form to relay the actual feelings and emotions that I experienced during that time. These are just a few of the many entries from my time in the woods. At the end of the two-year period, we moved to a new location, which ended my time in this particular place.

APPROACHING GOD

This morning, I woke up at 7:00 a.m. and felt a surge of heaviness. I rolled over and went back to sleep. At 11:30 a.m., I got up and went to the woods. I cried and called to Chloe. Then I tried to talk to God. I expressed how I had lost the trust I once had. I didn't know where the spirit of God lived, and I was afraid to be vulnerable and get hurt again. I believed in the existence of Spirit, but that's really all I understood. Then I closed my eyes and just breathed. I asked Chloe where she was now, but nothing really came to me. I just sat in the quiet.

Then I followed the trail that led back to my house. I stopped at her tree. I put some snow around it so it would have moisture. I held the small trunk and told her to grow and give life to others. I kissed a branch and then went home.

LYING IN THE WOODS

I had an agitated feeling of needing to get out to the woods. I found a place where there was no snow, in the shelter of the unwavering Aspen trees.

I talked to Chloe and told her I wanted to grow with her, to know her and be with her. I meditated on things like courage, compassion, and increased sensitivity to the spiritual world. I just lay there in the quietness. I asked the trees and the earth to be with me. It started to snow lightly, and the snow felt good on my face. I sat up and looked out of the trees and up into the sky. The snow was light and gentle. I asked Chloe where she was, what she was doing today. I heard a bird calling from far away. Then two birds flew over my head, calling to each other. They did that a couple times.

As I was sitting there, I saw two long, slender stems of some kind of plant. They were standing together with nothing else around. I just kept watching them. It was funny, how they seemed to be talking to each other, but without words. One would lean in toward the other and then back out again. Spirits communicate without words, but through thoughts and feelings. Words don't provide enough vocabulary for the richness of their communication.

Then I thought that maybe they weren't communicating. Maybe they were just being together, just existing. As I watched the two stems, I thought that maybe that was how I would communicate with Chloe. It wouldn't always be important to have words, but just sit together.

On my return to the house, I stopped at her tree and talked to her. I thanked her for the words I had read about identity in her writings. I gathered up some snow and gave her tree a drink.

My very existence is my identity

~ CHLOe

FEAR OF GOING TO THE WOODS

I wanted to go to the woods this afternoon, but I had some kind of fear about doing it. I guess maybe I was afraid it would make me sad, that I would feel more pain because Chloe should be there. I didn't want to let my fear be my guide, so I went. I wandered around—off the trail, on the trail. I sat on a rock and talked and thought. My sadness has increased, or maybe it's just that I can feel it now a little deeper without all the distractions of work. I have more disbelief; she should be home now. I wake up. I get out of bed. I move myself forward, and yet, I feel so much more consistent pain, although not debilitating. I guess I'll not try to chase it away. I'll just embrace and accept it. I'll keep taking those steps forward, no matter how small they may be.

As I was sitting there, deep in thought and tears, I suddenly fell off of that rock. I started laughing, looking around to see if anyone from the nearby trail might have seen me. I got up and headed back to the house, thinking about the interesting ebb and flow of the emotions of grief.

SOME PEACE

I went to the woods again today. I sat on Chloe's blanket and talked to her awhile. Then I meditated to clear my mind. I lay down directly on the earth and felt the energy of the ground under me and the sky above. I initially found myself in this position mostly because my body felt too weak to hold myself erect. I was unsettled, with the feeling of pieces floating out of sync with one another. But what I discovered as I lay there is that the earth was bringing me some kind of gift, a kind of energy that was pulling me back together. In brokenness, as I lay on the earth, life was being drawn into my body and spirit and was grounding my unraveled pieces.

I fell in and out of sleep. I could hear the wind around me, but I was in a sheltered place. I found peace there.

THE EARTH AND A BUTTERFLY

I took my rain poncho to lay on the ground because it was a little wet. I put Chloe's blanket on top of the poncho. The plants had grown so much with the recent rain. I just sat and looked at everything around me, and I listened. Everything smelled good. I felt peace. I talked to Chloe. I sat in silence. I lay down on the blanket and felt the earth under me. I felt peaceful and happy, even though I was missing Chloe. I got up and started to walk down the path. I had found a note that Chloe wrote that said she'd found a place in the woods to build a labyrinth. I have been looking for that place. I think I found it.

When I was walking home, I passed Chloe's tree and I said, "Fly, Chloe, fly." I wanted to give her the freedom to do what she needed to do. At the moment I said that, a large yellow butterfly circled around my head and flew down the path in front of me. When I got just about to my house, it flew out toward me again and then past Oscar, Chloe's dog and then into the woods.

She flew.

FROM BROKENNESS TO PEACE

I slept until 4:30 a.m. and then woke and just stared at the ceiling, painful pressure searing through me. I didn't want to die; I just didn't know how to live. Finally, I fell asleep. When I woke up again, I felt better. But then my heart was like gathering storm clouds, and I was crying. I grabbed Chloe's blanket and went to the woods. I cried all the way. I sat on a rock and rolled her blanket up and held it. It is the closest I can get to feel like I'm holding her. The tears would not stop. It felt like everything inside of me was breaking. I knew I had to just let the tears come and not try to stop them. After some time, the crying stopped. I felt calm. I asked her if she could sit in silence with me. Then I lay down on her blanket and felt the earth under me. A breeze was blowing through the young Aspens, and their leaves sounded like a song. I was able to gather strength and let the pain melt a little. I always have this ache, but, in that moment, I felt content and peaceful, even happy.

ASPEN

I was quiet in the woods today, just watching, listening and being. Everything was still and warm. I moved my blanket out of the sun and took my long-sleeved shirt off and sat comfortably in my tank top, absorbing the sun. I asked Chloe where she was and where the spirits were. All of a sudden, a strong, cold wind blew in. It swirled around me with such force. I looked up to see if a storm was moving in, but there was nothing, really; only blue sky. Then it stopped. It slowed, and the sun came out. I fixated on a small Aspen during this time. It was being whipped everywhere, but still it stood, like it was giving itself to the storm, trusting that it would be OK. I wanted to be like that little Aspen.

OCTOBER 24, 2011

Dear Chloe,
        You left on October 24, 2010. I soon found this place between three trees. I came here because these are the woods you spent so much time in. I

came here because I needed to find you and resolve the challenging depth of life and death, the parts that end and the parts that continue. I listened to the wind, I felt the sun and watched the snow. I let the earth absorb my tears. My eyes saw more deeply. I heard the silence from which you emerged. I felt things I never had felt before. Pain was intense and peace was miraculous. It is here where my heart broke many times over, and here where I found some kind of order. Life became simpler and more profound. It was in November, 2010, when you asked me to learn your language, and I knew I would only be able to do that in solitude. You helped me understand that it was OK to be together in silence. And so the cords of love and connection have lengthened. Still, I would rather hold you in my arms than experience all the depth and soul expansion this year has brought. But your presence has come in ways that take my breath away. I can only be grateful. I don't suppose the ache or the tears will stop anytime soon, but one thing I do know is I am with you, and you are with me. I love you, sweet spirit child.

A New Tree

This week, a friend gave me a small tree and told me to do with it whatever I needed. Many trees had been planted for Chloe. I felt deeply honored by them and the people who planted them. Today I went to my place in the woods and planted this little tree for myself and my commitment to grow, not in the absence of pain or tears, but by letting them be with me in life. It was an incredibly peaceful day.

Two Years in the Woods

In my two years in the woods, I have gone from brokenness and heartache to peace, contentment, and balance. They haven't always been in this linear order but are quite random and usually unpredictable. Initially, I thought I would experience a progression in grief, from dark sorrow to some kind of healing and light where the pain would lessen with time. That was not the case. As if stepping off of a railroad track, I needed to shed the idea that healing would come in a straight line and right on schedule. There was no "conductor" to dictate my path. I just had to trust that my heart knew what it needed and I had to honor it in every moment. Movement forward wasn't as much about diminished tears and sorrow as how I responded to them. At first, when I found myself engulfed in tears, I saw these times as dreadful storms. But soon I began to observe that tears brought peace, and even joy. I learned to greet the tears as an old friend, knowing that this sadness wasn't a terminal condition, just a moment.

As I have come into this new way of being, I feel myself pulled in a new direction, having a dual experience. One is grieving the loss of Chloe's physical presence and the other is getting to know where Chloe is and who she is now. Her message is becoming louder and stronger. "Be with me now, know the person I am in the present." As a parent, it is often difficult to see who our children truly are when they're standing right in front of us, but I knew that part of my work was to know Chloe in whatever form she took, and to accept her.

I have learned much from Chloe and from the intuitive healers in my life. Questions that I thought were not supposed to have answers have been answered. There are still tears, but I go to the woods to meet her and learn what is here for me and her now. There is a newfound release in letting her continue to fulfill her purpose and for me to have a deeper sense of my own. As we anticipate moving out of our house and onto our new property, it may be time to close the chapter on "the place between three trees" in order to find a new place of healing and hope at Dream Valley Ranch.

CHAPTER 3

Letters From Rohini

ON OCTOBER 25, 2010, ROHINI Kanniganti courageously and compassion-
ately stepped into my life and into my space. It is always a risk to approach
someone in the throes of tragedy and loss. You must be able to read that person carefully, as he or she may or may not want you there. I have always been
the one to stay away, afraid of saying or doing the wrong thing, all the while
protecting myself from any painful encounter. Rohini's words and actions are
a demonstration of one of the many ways to walk with someone in grief.

Dear Cindy,

*I don't know where you are physically, so I am e-mailing. My heart is
breaking. I can imagine shock covers you like a blanket, and that there are
terrible things to look after. I offer myself to you as community member,
friend and a healing resource. I am here to sit with you in your deepest grief
and hold you. I am here whenever you are ready to receive more support. I
will be watching out for you, and will be gently blessing your every step. In
the midst of crisis, we are often repulsed by food, drink and sleep. Please eat,
drink and sleep. Please reach for help. I am here holding love and caring for
you in my heart.*
with love
Rohini

Dear Rohini,
  Thank you for your beautiful, comforting words.
Chloe was such a sweetheart. Now she will be my
sweet spirit child. I will take you up on those hugs.
Cindy

Cindy Brave,
  I am so glad you have given yourself this time to let your body and
mind grieve and your spirit to touch Chloe's. I am hosting a healing circle
at my home sometime this week to give us a chance to be with each other
from our hearts, processing together what this tragedy has brought to us.
My intention is that people can share when the spirit moves them to share,
or silently benefit from the sharing of others. I am hoping that as people
give voice to their experience, that something of meaningfulness emerges. It
may not, but I imagine that we will all benefit tremendously from being
together in this way.
  I would love to have you participate, if you are drawn. My full un-
derstanding in this invitation is that you can say no, very simply. You will
feel our loving energy regardless.
With Love
Rohini

Dear Rohini,
  This sounds beautiful. We just returned from Alamosa where we at-
tended a second memorial service for Chloe. It really was almost over-
whelming for us to go through it again. We are home now and taking no
calls or visitors so we can just fall apart as we need to. I just can't handle
being with a group of people right now, but I would love to talk to you in-
dividually at some point. I can't seem to get myself out of the house, except

to walk in the woods. It seems I just want to spend my days walking and talking to Chloe. Perhaps toward the end of the week we could get together. I feel your
love. thank you.
Cindy

Dear Cindy,
    I am so glad you are back at work. Sitha and her friends are beside themselves with joy about your return to the classroom.
    Sending you love, and the presence of breath in painful moments.
Rohini

Dear Rohini,
    Thank you so much. The love of my students was overwhelming in a positive way.
Cindy

Cindy Radiant,
    I've been thinking about "the other side of pain." When I have sat with my pain and don't rush it (it won't be rushed, it has the consistency of jello, on good days), I do get to the other side. But which side? Now this is a fascinating question I've been sitting with.
    My wonderful friend Laura, a psychologist, described something really interesting in a workshop for fire survivors (last year) we were facilitating together. She was recalling a time in her life when she was in her sister's home and her sister's child was undergoing some very complicated heart surgery. A friend of her sister's called on the

phone...Laura answered...the friend asked, "how is she doing?"
Laura answered, "Well, on the surface she is OK. Underneath that
she is not OK. Underneath that she is a wreck. And underneath that
she is really, really OK."
    This for me is a simple and profound description of our lives.
    The top layer of Okay-ness is the layer of functioning...the social
engagement... And I think that it is a state of holding, waiting, tolerat-
ing. The bottom layer is the sense of oneness...my pain and your pain.
Interestingly, the deeper and more searing the pain, the more I am able to
experience a sense of oneness after being with it.
    But in my experience, none of this is permanent. All these states
seem to be constantly in flux, interacting and mixing. I am still sit-
ting in awe, scared out of my mind, but in absolute awe of this pro-
cess. What happens when we are swallowed by our brokenness, un-
able to move? Sitting with it and moving slowly through it already
implies some resilience, rootedness, resource. Where is that streaming
from? What happens when we do a "spiritual bypass," i.e. skip over the
brokenness like a pebble over our thoughts and feelings, and attribute
everything to the great mystery of life, God? Are we in this place capable
of experiencing the oneness?
    Well,
    I'm done now, you can wake up.
    Ha ha. bedtime, and a prayer.
with love
Rohini

Dear Rohini,
    You have described the experience of loss so perfectly. It splits you wide
open and there can be nothing to hide. I don't understand how it can be
such a "soul-ripping" and "soul-deepening" experience all at the same
time, but it is. Yesterday I lay on the forest floor and the snow fell lightly

on me. I felt surrounded by spirits and I was grounded, centered, and peaceful just sitting with Chloe. I am working hard on learning the language of the spirit world. I learned yesterday that sometimes it is enough just to sit with her, with no communication at all. But in the evening I felt a wave of shock come back at me and I fell into disbelief. Whatever presents itself at the moment that is what I have to walk straight through. I'm finding that having the courage to walk through the middle of my pain without rushing it gets me to the other side.
Cindy

Cindy,
I am moved to such stillness as I reread what you wrote. so honored, so honored and filled with tears. a sudden image of St. Francis of Assisi, feeding birds in silence and complete softness.
Rohini

Dear Darling Cindy,
Sorry I've been out of the loop. I speak frequently of you these days, for instance last night at my women's group. I would love to have you join if you wish…and if that is something that would be lovely for you. They already know how amazing you are and how I value our friendship. This week and part of last, I've been the only doc in clinic, so I've been quite busy. I'm glad to be busy, there's something deeply therapeutic about dissolving pain and self-doubt into service and connection. I will be gone the next two weeks starting Monday afternoon after clinic. I would love to walk with you then.
Here's an excerpt from "The Brain that Changes Itself" by Normal Doidge. This part is about how we process loss… It is preceded by a discussion about how we hang on to our broken heart in loss: "Often

such people cannot move on because they cannot yet grieve; the thought of living without the one they love is too painful to bear. In neuroplastic terms, if the person is to begin a new relationship without baggage, each must first rewire billions of connections in their brains. The work of mourning is piecemeal, Freud noted; though reality tells us our loved one is gone, "its orders cannot be obeyed at once." We grieve by calling up one memory at a time, reliving it, and then letting go. At a brain level, we are turning on each of the neural networks that were wired together to form our perception of the person, experiencing the memory with exceptional vividness, and then saying good-bye one network at a time. In grief, we learn to live without the one we love, but the reason this lesson is so hard is that we must first unlearn the idea that the person exists and can still be relied on."

I thought of you, you sitting in the woods, you walking down into the basement with Chloe's clothes, your process of such beautiful integrity these last months. And I thought again, how smart she is. How true to herself.
love
Rohini

Cindy
   We found a lovely heart rock today outside school and thought of you.
love
Rohini

Cindy,
   I am scared to ask you something, but I will anyway... The intention is for healing for everyone, but it may come across to you as gross

insensitivity. May I use a part of what you've written in my presentation. It is an exquisite and alive description of the trauma process. please please please feel free to say no and forgive me for causing pain if I did.
love
Rohini

Rohini,
If anything I have ever said in our conversations can be used to help or heal others, I give it to you freely. In February I visited a Medium. It was an amazing visit. At the end she thought I would be spending part of my life helping people to heal. I really didn't get that then and I still don't. I only see myself as trying to survive this loss with some deepening of my spirit. But it is a natural response to now want to come running to anyone in pain. I guess time will tell how it all evolves.
Cindy

Cindy
This journey of yours has lighted my path. I don't know why and how... I have been clear, sustainedly. Each conversation with you has somehow propelled me to a new level. It has beautifully paralleled the incredible integrative effect of my own trauma therapy work, which has been very different from the psychotherapy I've done in the past. I bow before this budding friendship, and this internal sense of divine partnership with you.
I am working on a new paradigm of healing with a wonderful spirit based psychologist, of which a huge part is education. Perhaps this is why you are in my life as you are. Let us feel into this path together. In the

meantime, I will direct you to the work of Dan Siegel, Peter Levine, Pat Ogden and Bassel Vander Kolk. Most important is anything you can read about the power of attachment.
love
Rohini

Cindy Beautiful,
   At my presentation I read aloud a piece of your email while protecting your identity. People referred to it specifically after the talk was done, that it helped them realize they were not alone.
   Thank you. Your writing helped a lot of people, and others through them. Please keep writing.
love
Rohini

CHAPTER 4

Holidays

WE ARE OFTEN ADVISED TO find a "new normal." This will happen without you attempting to find or create it. It finds you. The holidays were approached in different ways. We went on trips, planted trees, hiked, spent the day as a family, or spent the day alone. We were together, and we were apart. We cried and we laughed. On the first Christmas, we traveled to avoid the gaping hole. But we cried on our trip because Chloe was absent from us. We also laughed and didn't concern ourselves with traditions. Holidays have brought anxiety, fear, sorrow, happiness, love, and anticipation. I was surprised to find that there was no way to predict what a particular holiday would hold even over the passage of time. For example, my birthday in the first year was one of experiencing Chloe's presence in a powerful way, while my birthday in the third year left me longing for her hand-made gifts. As I approached a certain holiday, I might find myself feeling joy with no apparent grief, only to collapse into tears the day before or three days after. If I passed through a special day and I had been fine and the day had been good, I found myself surprised, saying, "Hey, wasn't I supposed to cry or something?"

After experiencing many holidays without Chloe, the most important thing I have learned is to let go of all expectations about what the holidays will hold. There is no way to anticipate the experience. Instead I try to just be in each moment.

GIVING AND RECEIVING

Giving and receiving gifts has always brought me joy. I love shopping for my kids, thinking about what would make them happy on each holiday. The end of selecting and giving gifts to Chloe is a great loss. No longer receiving her handmade gifts and cards to me is also a great loss. Today I was in a store and aching because I could not buy her anything. I suddenly heard her say, "it's OK, I don't need those anymore." The message continued as I was guided back through all the times of her life, through all of the gifts that made her happy. The soap collection, erasers, hats, backpacking equipment. With each stage of her life, she enjoyed something different. I finally understood that gifts for Chloe now had shifted from material items to gifts of the heart. "What would really make Chloe happy now?" I think the answer is for me to be happy, to engage in love and connection with those close to me. Also, to go to the woods and just be with her. Making that mental and spiritual shift has brought a deeper meaning to the holidays.

NEW GIFTS

Today was my first birthday without Chloe. I didn't know how this day would be. She never missed doing something special for me, usually in the form of a quirky, homemade gift. I began talking to her about it as I drove into town on my way to work. I asked her if she could still give me a gift. Then a big truck pulled out with shamrocks all over it. Shamrocks have come to be a sign that she is around. She had a small one tattooed on the inside of her wrist. Herm called her "Clover" more than he called her by her own name. I laughed and said thank you.

In the evening, I met Herm, Hope, and Dillon for a birthday meal. Up to this time, I was carrying pain, in some form, every day. Even though moments of happiness were working to interweave themselves into my heart, I could always feel it. I met my family and then went to the bathroom to wash my hands. Something suddenly washed over me. A feeling of complete peace and joy. I felt no pain but only happiness. I just stood there reveling in the mystery. There were no tangible possessions, just a gift of the heart.

CHLOE'S BIRTHDAY, YEAR ONE

I woke up at 2:00 a.m., the hour of Chloe's birth. I thought about her transition into this world, which wasn't an easy one. She clearly had second thoughts about what she was getting herself into. But I am grateful she made it. She gave me warmth, she made me smile. She taught me how to care about someone besides myself. As a child, she could never take a nap alone and often lay right on top of me. She was quiet, but when we were alone together, she talked nonstop. There was so much she wanted to know.

Later, in the quiet of the morning, I looked out over the mountains and talked to her. I felt a calmness. Learning to be with her in this new way is more than I expected and yet holds a certain sadness. I never felt I could give Chloe all that she needed in this life, but in the process of trying, we somehow developed a bond. The bond is the reason for the tears and the heartache. I continue on, because I am determined to grow with her. I will embrace the pain, knowing what it is: the measure of our love.

CHLOE'S BIRTHDAY, YEAR TWO

I've been thinking about Chloe's birthday this week, but it hasn't bothered me much. I remember the gift she gave me this year, on my first birthday without her: pure joy and the absence of pain, even if only for a couple hours. It was the first time I had ever been without pain since losing her. I've been thinking about what she would really want now. It would probably be my own happiness.

I went to get groceries, a routine event. I walked past the aisle of gluten-free cookies and saw her favorite ones. The cold reality of her absence just hit me, and I started to cry, hoping I wouldn't see anyone I knew. I tried to hold back my feelings, but it made me agitated at everyone around me. I saw the birthday cakes; I cried again. This was the day that I would be getting ready for her birthday. This week was when I would have bought her a gift. But there was nothing.

I took off of work and spent the day alone in the woods. It was one of the most peaceful, light-filled days I have had. On other days, I have been a train wreck. Sometimes working too hard to create a new normal only delays the grief. Accepting that tears are a part of my new landscape has helped me to walk directly into the holiday. I have found myself digging for a more meaningful experience rather than just letting the years repeat themselves without reflection.

CHLOE'S BIRTHDAY, YEAR THREE

Dear Chloe,

I woke up the night before, somewhere around 1:30 a.m., thinking about your birth. Thank you for staying with me on this earth for twenty years, even though I wanted more. That was an awesome day. You were so beautiful, and I loved you immediately. I never stopped. I have a scar to remind me that you really came into my life. You have been in my life now for twenty-three years. I still love you with all my heart. I miss you that much too. May 16th approaches now with some pressure on my heart. It did not take me completely down this year, but I missed having this day be one of happy anticipation, celebrating you, picking out a gift, making you feel special. I didn't know what to get you; I still don't. Our family breakfast was fun; your absence in that fifth chair around the table is becoming a little more normal, although still empty. We were all here during the day and then Dillon went to a concert with his friends at night. I was glad that Dillon could go to the concert. It is good to honor, remember and be with each other and with you, but it is also good to focus on ourselves. I read the book Growing Up in Heaven. *Are you going to school? I think you might be in music school. I hope so. I miss you, Chloe. I love you. Happy Birthday.*

CHRISTMAS, YEAR ONE

I couldn't even comprehend this holiday. I would stand and stare at the TV, listening to the usual holiday materialism commercials. I just didn't get it, it made no sense. Why would I want "things?" What are these people doing? Was I an alien now? No one in our family gave any thought, desire or energy to a tree, decorating or celebrating this year. It is almost as if we didn't know it was happening. We planned a trip to Ohio to be with extended family, mostly because we knew we couldn't be home. We stayed in a hotel instead of with family so we could have the space we needed to navigate this unpredictable holiday. I mostly cried on this trip and throughout the holiday. That didn't mean it was the wrong decision. I would have cried at home as well. It was a needed distraction and being with people, although a little foggy, was helpful at times.

CHRISTMAS, YEAR TWO

One day I felt a twinge of holiday spirit and bought a wreath, put lights on it, and hung it on my door. A couple weeks into December I found myself driving to a tree farm attempting to pick out a "Charlie Brown" tree, small and understated. I became overwhelmed with the memories of taking our kids to the tree farm every year and stood in the middle of the lot sobbing, but not leaving. A man came to check on me and realized I was crying. I decided not to hide and told him my story. He gave me a hug and I bought the little tree. On the way home I was peaceful and reflected on my experience at the tree farm and the goodness of humanity I seem to encounter everywhere I go.

The house was empty when I got home that evening. I turned on some music and put one string of lights on the little tree. I felt quietly happy and peaceful. Herm thanked me for it. Dillon arrived home, opened the door and started laughing, "We have a BUSH for a Christmas tree!" I laughed. We laughed. We had a tree.

SAN DIEGO

Still unable to comprehend actually being home for Christmas on this second year we planned a trip to San Diego, hoping the sun and the distance would help us to find a new way. A few days before coming here, I lost my appetite. I didn't feel sick; I just had no desire to eat. Soon, I started feeling kind of ill, so I decided it would be good to make myself eat. Once I started eating again, I felt better.

It was good to get away and feel the sunshine. I enjoyed biking the most. One evening, I took a walk along the shore. I soon found myself sitting on a bench, crying, and couldn't stop. Then I kept walking. The thing I am aware of is that I can't feel beauty or inspiration the way I used to. I mostly see things, but I can't feel them the way I once did. I enjoyed the whale-watching cruise and there was laughter, but I also found myself staring out across the ocean. When the whales emerged, I just watched with no feeling. I feel half dead and half alive. Is this a normal way to feel? Will it pass? Then I sat with Hope and Dillon and we laughed. We had an evening meal looking out across the water. I felt happy and peaceful.

There was a seagull that kept visiting us. We named her Rebecca. I can only keep trying to move forward.

CHRISTMAS, YEAR THREE

This is the third Christmas. It has been very different. I feel like I have basically ignored the whole season and at the same time returned to some traditions. Early in December, I put a red tablecloth on my table. That was it. Not the usual breaking out the decorations and listening to music. Then I pushed it away, with some intermittent sadness.

Sometimes I wonder if I will survive. I am struggling to type a complete sentence without multiple errors. Focus is difficult. I can feel the holiday more than last year. I want to participate, but I just hit a brick wall with every thought of holiday traditions. I'm not emotional or crying, but I'm swirling. I feel like Dorothy in The Wizard of Oz *when her house is taken up in the tornado. I feel like a freak. I can't participate in the holidays. I watch people around me fully immersed and celebrating. To them, it is joy; to me, it is pain. There is pressure in my heart and stomach.*

It was in this month of December when we were in the process of closing on our new property and would be moving after Christmas. Although we had not yet moved, Herm and Hope went over to the new property and cut a Christmas tree down. Hope was happy. Herm told me that if I just went over there, it would help me feel better. Later in the afternoon, Hope and I went over to decorate it. There it was, a tree towering into the cathedral ceiling, in an empty house. I felt sadness that Chloe wasn't there. I knew how excited she would have been. I have not been able to go down into the basement and get the boxes of decorations at our

Sundance house, where Chloe lived with us. I actually thought I never wanted to see them again. But Herm had brought them into the new house. When we got there, there was so much light streaming into the room. I felt some healing and happiness. Hope and I were even able to laugh at some of the decorations. Then Hope called me to the kitchen window. There was a herd of elk grazing in the back pasture. They were strong and gentle. A true gift.

MOTHER'S DAY, YEAR ONE
I went to the woods with Chloe's blanket. I cried deeply. We went to my sister's house for a family Mother's Day gathering. This was not a good choice for me. I was on someone else's timeline, not wanting to disappoint my family. I wasn't ready to be there without Chloe. All of the holiday happiness was more than I could bear. I am a mother, I was being celebrated, and so very grateful for Hope and Dillon. But I am the mother of three, not two. I could see that it was also difficult for Hope and Dillon. I wanted to scoop them up and run home.

MOTHER'S DAY, YEAR TWO
I woke up at 6:00 a.m. and stared at the ceiling and remembered it was Mother's Day. I started to cry and tried to go back to sleep so I wouldn't feel it. I couldn't sleep, so I got up at 7 and went to the woods. I just let everything out and cried. I would stop and breathe and then cry again. I sat there for a long time, sometimes with my eyes open and sometimes with them closed. Then I went back to the house.

Hope gave me a necklace she made with a shell she saved from San Diego. She wanted me to remember that good times that are being made, even though there are still hard times.

MOTHER'S DAY, YEAR THREE
I hadn't given a thought to the upcoming holiday. I felt nothing, really, until Saturday night. Then I felt a heaviness, a sadness descend, but I went to bed. Dillon came into my room and made me laugh. I woke up at 3:30 a.m. and knew

it was Mother's Day. I didn't want to face it. No banging in the kitchen as the kids attempted to make one of their signature breakfasts which always included strawberries. I wanted to go back to sleep and not wake up until Monday so I could just skip the whole day. In fact, I was thinking how nice it would be if all holidays would just be discontinued.

I woke up at 6:30 am. I was OK. I had some tea and looked out at the horses. I went to feed them, and then I started working in the arena, trying to create a drainage system so the water could run off. There is something that happens when you work with the earth. I was still, quiet, watching the patterns of the delicate streams trickling into the small, shallow grooves in the earth. Then I pushed myself physically to rake gravel. I saw Hope coming toward me. When she got to me, she hugged me and cried. I just held her, knowing that these were days that she and Chloe would have done together. She had made a beautiful necklace for me with Chloe's beads and a picture of Chloe, Oscar, and a dream catcher. On the back it read, "It's not life that matters. It's the courage that you bring to it." I loved that, because I feel myself having to bring courage into every moment.

Then I took Hope and showed her how to halter the horses and she started working with Ace. She spent time grooming him, twice. She cleaned out the stalls and paddocks. I saw happiness return to her. And then there was some laughter when Dillon rode off into the woods on the ATV with Hope sitting behind him. We knew they were going to get stuck in the mud, which they did and had to walk back.

EASTER, YEAR ONE

With Chloe gone and perspectives on life shifting, do I just throw out the holidays or decide what they really mean to me? The general idea in the Christian tradition is that there is death followed by life. I like that; I think I'd like to hold on to that idea. In the secular world, I think I'm done with the Easter Bunny. I think the egg has some meaning in "the seed of life." I can probably keep that one but I'll have to explore it a little further. Family gatherings are always a good thing. In the physical world, it is a time of new life: the flowers, the trees, the animals, and maybe for myself as well. This seems to be where I want to focus this holiday.

I have a new way of thinking about Easter and how I want to celebrate it. First, I am going to try to be more focused on signs of life, in the earth and in myself. It doesn't mean I have to push the sorrow out, but just look for life. Second, when Lent begins each year, instead of giving something up, I'd like to add something into my life that would be very nurturing and provide me with some real meaning.

I have developed a new mantra for these holiday times, to help me anticipate light instead of dark:

- What goodness will I receive on this day?
- What goodness will I give on this day?
- What tears of love will I shed?
- How will I honor myself and Chloe?

CHAPTER 5

Anger

I'D LIKE TO SAY THAT anger wasn't part of my experience, that I could somehow find an acceptance of this loss without it. But it wasn't so. I grew up with the idea that people were "children of God." But after losing Chloe, I was in excruciating pain. If I was a child, then shouldn't God be operating in a "parent-type" role? As a parent, if one of my children were in pain, I would do everything in my power to come to them and bring healing. If they cut their finger, I wouldn't just stand and watch and tell them I loved them. This would be a form of neglect and abuse. I felt like an abused child, afraid of my parent. Reserved and tentative to even come close.

When anger presented itself, the timing was never my choice. How I chose to deal with it *was* my choice. There is always the option of pushing it down and away. But as with all of my emotions of grief, I somehow invited each one to take its rightful place and run its course. I observed that after an episode of anger I felt purged, cleansed. Not angry or clutching to it anymore. The admission that I was angry that I lost Chloe was crucial, even in the times of recognizing that it may have had its divine purpose. It will never be "alright," even when I am feeling the deepest peace and immersed in love.

Anger is really deep sadness. When you lift up the lid of anger and uncover it, you see the very deep loss underneath. It is sometimes hard to differentiate sadness from anger except that it has the additional component of feeling control-or loss of it. In sadness I tend to cry. In anger I want to break all my dishes. There is a kind of action attached to it, even if it is only screaming.

It also allows your deepest emotion of loss and love to come forth, honoring yourself by not silencing the pain.

My anger wanted out and I let it. In time it stopped asking for space in my life. I don't think it was just the passage of time, but rather the work I continued to do to love deeper, to strategically connect to Chloe, my family and my universal tribe. I just became propelled to live more fully and I didn't want to be robbed of that. It was important for me to record my anger in my journal. It somehow finished the emotion and experience, not allowing any residue to linger.

SCREAMING

Yesterday, I was OK at school. It was a day of holiday festivities, but I just ignored it for most of the day. By the last hour, I could feel it creeping up on me. I just wanted to get out of there. As I was driving down Nineteenth Street, I started to cry. All I could do was call out Chloe's name over and over. Then I felt angry and started on a rant about this stupid life-and-death setup. At the end, I just screamed. I hadn't done that before, and what came out of my mouth kind of surprised me. I didn't hold anything back. No one was there, and I didn't have to worry about alarming anyone. It's like having an open wound on your arm and someone brushes past it. Your reaction is much stronger than if you had no wound because it triggers the pain again. I felt washed out after that, but eventually better. It comes down to this. I want to express anger in appropriate ways and not turn away from it. But I don't want to let my loss of Chloe turn me into an angry person.

LETTER TO GOD

God, I thought I was done with these feelings, I thought they were just a stage I went through several months back. But here I am again. I feel so utterly abandoned by you. You did not take care of me or protect me the way I have cared for, loved, and protected my own children. How can you possibly care for me and watch the heartache and the pain? How could you set life up like this? You seem big and far away. You are a perfect, flawless being who doesn't have to participate in the life you set up. You don't have to hurt and cry. How can I possibly relate to you? How can I even get near you? Am I angry? Yes, but mostly hurt.

INDIFFERENCE, ANGER, AND SADNESS

I have felt this growing indifference about Chloe's death. Comments that emerge from me are, "Oh, well, whatever. It's not up to me. I have no say in my life. I'm walking. . .living, breathing. . . living." There has been no intense emotion of sadness or anger, just a flat indifference. I walked past Chloe's picture feeling numb. Later, I felt a growing need to just lie on my yoga mat and breathe. I started crying so deeply, and I knew what I had been masking: a deep, shattering sadness. I cried, and it felt better. It happened again as I was going to my horse-riding lesson, I tried to understand this. What was I protecting? I tried to be more honest with myself and I found that indifference masks anger but is more acceptable. The more I felt what was dwelling inside me, the more anger I found. I guess I thought I should be done with that. But it was a different kind of anger. I feel like I've been tricked. Life says, "Invest deeply in your children, your relationships. Find ways to make them grow and sink deep into your heart. Oh, but oops, forgot to tell you that after you have given your heart and soul to them, they will be ripped away." So it all seems so pointless, knowing that I really have nothing I can count on. How do I trust in anything? I can't make myself vulnerable to that raping pain again.

Monday, day four of tears. I don't understand this. It is unusual for it to linger like this. I go through times when I feel so sheltered, like I don't really even know that Chloe's gone. But in these past days, I have felt all of its sharpness; every piercing reality grips me. I am either crying or wanting to scream at people. I don't want to be the one who has been hurt. Why does everyone one else get their happiness? In the past few days, I have received messages from friends who care deeply about me and are staying with me through all of this. Still, I feel so angry. No matter how much people care, hurt, and cry, they don't have to lose their child. I do. They can still have rich times with all of their children; I feel like a freak. I am not alone and yet it is a solo journey.

REDIRECTED ANGER, YEAR THREE

My anger no longer seems to be directed at God—or anyone, for that matter. It is anger existing alone. These feelings are lessening now, and there are greater and longer moments of either sadness or a deepening sense of divine purpose. Anger doesn't serve much of a purpose anymore except to ease my moments of grief, but they are infrequent now. As I continue to gain an understanding of where Chloe is, I can feel her place in my life. Greater peace and love are beginning to replace anger.

MELTING ANGER, YEAR FOUR

I feel my anger melting. As a greater perspective starts opening up and Chloe has begun to show me who she is, where she is, and her new purpose, my energy has shifted to being with her where she is and taking a deeper dive into my own spirit. I am being propelled onto a new plane. It is rather unfamiliar but full of love and light. I can bring my tears there, but I have found I don't really need my anger anymore.

CHAPTER 6

Forgiveness

IN COLIN TIPPING'S BOOK, *RADICAL Forgiveness*, he says that people who are grieving need to be able to explore forgiveness honestly and deeply. Pat answers will not suffice for those having to deal with painful forgiveness.

I began wondering about my own relationship with forgiveness and decided a little reflection on the whole idea might benefit me. I sat on my bedroom floor, lit a candle, listened to Pachelbel's Canon, and brought myself to a state of meditation and prayer. Uncluttering my mind always helps me to hear and gain greater understanding. I closed my eyes and commenced talking to Chloe. I released her from this physical plane so that she might fulfill her purpose and find ultimate happiness. I acknowledged that we do not exist for each other and yet remain deeply connected. I scanned my heart to see what came up when I thought about forgiveness.

I am still not clear on my own definition of forgiveness in this context. I don't know how I'm supposed to feel or what I'm supposed to "do." And yet, I don't feel the need to arrive at any conclusion.

I did not do much journaling or therapeutic work around forgiveness. It wasn't a component that was out in front. I was more consumed with missing Chloe and finding ways to help myself gain a sense of peace and happiness. I don't think I was initially aware that it even had any place in my grieving process. In time, I felt it needed some attention. I first had to look carefully at who or what it is I am unable to forgive. To most, it would seem, the obvious: the teenager who took Chloe from this world. Although he did not intend to hurt her, his irresponsible driving resulted in her death. Forgiveness just seemed rather neutral. I didn't really forgive him, but neither did I feel a festering anger or need for vengeance. I just didn't think about him. I didn't even know what forgiveness meant in this context. People made comments about how our family did a great thing in forgiving him, but I didn't really; I just moved on and didn't hang on to his destructive action. A friend said to me, "he is not yours to deal with. He will have to deal with himself." Maybe that in itself is forgiveness-focusing myself forward to do what I needed most without getting caught in the snare of an event I could not change. Initially, I was just consumed with my grief. The day before the sentencing for this young man, I received a message through a medium and spiritual guide who first contacted Chloe in February, 2011. We had not communicated since that time. She knew nothing about the date of the sentencing, but on June 13, 2011, the day before the sentencing, she sent me this email:

"I have meant to write since we last met. I feel I must convey to you that Chloe wants you to send that boy your love, as hard as it may be, it will set you free, and him, as well as helping her. She expresses that she has been working to help him from the other side and will appreciate it, if and when you find it in yourself, to continue here the work she is doing on the other side for him. I hope this message does not cause you pain, but I felt you would want me to share anything that I was getting without filters."

We received several apologetic messages from him, and at that point, it ceased to be my focus. Was that forgiving him? His actions will never be all right or good, but that is for him to work out. I feel strongly that it was Chloe, herself, who propelled me out of that place and on to the real work that I needed to do. Not allowing bitterness to dwell within was the only way to bring peace and honor my spirit.

The few times I journaled about forgiveness were directed more at a higher entity—God, the one with the "so-called" power. I needed an apology or an explanation. Of course I got neither. But as I sat with my questions, I was somehow moving toward regaining love—the love of God. Not because of the biblical idea of God as love, or because I had been given this message my entire life, but because there were new experiences that were now coming to me in the midst of my search. It was a message of love that came quite apart from any holy book or sermon received in church. It was a truth that was becoming my own, in its purest form.

WHO NEEDS FORGIVENESS

I hear people making reference to forgiveness in the context of Chloe's death. Some are angered themselves, even to the point of vengeance. Others think it is wonderful the way I am able to forgive. Really? Did I say that? Assumptions are made without information. Still, I wonder if I am ignoring this forgiveness thing. Am I pretending that I'm not angry because it may be too emotionally charged? It just feels somewhat pointless to give any energy to something that will change nothing.

So, who needs forgiveness? Anyone at all? I suddenly realized that it was actually God. Although it seemed ludicrous that a divine being would need to be forgiven, I still needed some kind of resolution. This became clear by my refusal to talk to God in any form. My "I'm here but you're going to have to make the first move" attitude revealed that I was actually angry. What I had experienced just wasn't my definition of love and wasn't that the whole point of a God? Why couldn't a divine being care enough about me to prevent this pain from touching me?

GRANDMOTHER'S SONG

When I was a child, my grandmother taught me a song in German, "Gott ist die Liebe." I used to like to sing it, but had not thought about, or sung, it in years. I woke up one morning after losing Chloe and I was singing this song in German. This was shortly after the time I was exploring what forgiveness meant to me. Later that day, it was still going through my head, and I thought, that's strange. I wonder where that came from? I just let it go, but it kept coming back. All of a sudden, I said, "God is love. God loves even me," which was the main line of the song. I stopped. I've been struggling with who God is, my feelings of abandonment, and total confusion about the love of God. Then I woke up singing that song. I sat with all of this, and then I knew (with my usual skepticism lingering in the back of my mind): my grandmother had come to me and helped me to know that God is love and does love me. It is still hard to grasp, but it had to be that song in German or I wouldn't have known it was her. I think she was trying to help me.

I was suddenly aware of my eternal connection to my grandmother. The fact that, after all these years, she was still trying to help me, brought tears to my eyes. This made me aware at how, when those we love die, they make efforts to stay connected with us but we are generally "sleeping" or doubtful and we miss their messages.

If Only You Knew

It seemed that a turning process had begun. I turned to face, only slightly, in the direction of God, but still untrusting.

One day as I sat with Cheryl, she said, "I think it's time for you to deal with God." Not the words I wanted to hear. I liked the distance, and I was being introduced to many spirit helpers that had become an amazing part of this journey. However, I knew I should give this suggestion some effort. This didn't really send me running into the arms of God, but it led me to one question: Who are you? The answer: "If only you knew."

The next day, "My Sweet Lord" played on the radio, and I realized I longed for the divine, but in a totally new and different way. Everything had to be scrapped so I could truly see what was before me. This did not happen quickly, but the phrase "if only you knew" kept coming at me and taking form. The rest of that statement manifested in the days and months to follow. "If only you knew . . . how much I love you." Healing and forgiveness, then, was not solely about technique or practice, but about allowing myself to be loved and to know love. Losing Chloe made me feel unloved, unprotected, unsafe, untrusting. Opening my heart to pure love was scary, and I felt vulnerable. What if I embrace the divine and I am, again, hurt?

As I read over my journal entries and reflected on what was at the core of all of the emotions of forgiveness, I saw that it was really fear. In some way, forgiveness in any form, can bring a sense of danger, as if it could happen again if I let go. Keeping myself at a distance from forgiveness kept me safe from the pain. I could not cognitively resolve all the forgiveness issues and so it was easier to leave them for another day. In the end, I could see that forgiveness is all about trust, even when there is little understanding. Trust replaces fear.

I trust that there is a higher order to my life.
I trust that there is a purpose to the events
of my life.
I trust that all the players in my life are
perfectly cast.
I trust in what I cannot see or feel.
I trust that I am loved by God.
I trust my journey.

CHAPTER 7

Healing

HEALING? IS THAT WHAT I can hope for? When a wound heals, sometimes it closes and is no more; other times it heals and leaves a scar. Either way, there is restoration, repair. Does that mean I will "heal" from this deep, gaping wound festering around my heart? How could there be healing? How could that even be a word in this experience? But staying in my initial tortured state was not an option either. A wound closes in time. But the gap in my heart would never close, and I would never mend or be restored to the person I was. One definition of healing, according to Webster is "to patch up." Although Webster's definition of healing is appropriate for what happens after physical injury, it is not accurate for what happens in the context of emotional loss. So what does happen? The wound remains open, but it is that gap that propels you to dive deeper, that raw exposure that makes you long to transform. There is no waiting for the wound to close in order to step into life. Healing is holding and accepting the pain while allowing life to open up at the same time.

How Am I Now?
I reflect on queries asked of me by a friend, who wanted to know
where I was in my journey, and whether I had truly ventured
to the other side . . . I cannot fully answer this for it is a process.
Much is behind me, but there is still so much to overcome—
so much more to traverse—to reach that other side . . .
But I go forward—and into the river, I paddle, and I float in it,
and sometimes struggle to get to the other side as I strive to leave

behind what no longer serves . . . I am carried across in so many
ways—I am carried by Grace—my faithful boat—and I am carried
by the love and prayers and the support of blessed ones in my life.

—OLGA RASMUSSEN

For me, the question is more, "how am I in this moment?" If you see me dancing with exuberant joy, you might draw the conclusion that I have crossed the
bridge of pain and loss and have made it to the other side. On another day,
you might see me in deep collapse and become concerned that I am in such a
broken state. I have grown accustomed to all states of grief, and I don't panic
or become hostage to any moment. My experiences and emotions just weave
in and out of each other while I observe them, feel them, and honor them all.

One day as I was driving to my horse-riding lesson, I was thinking about
healing and felt something was coming to me, but I couldn't explain it. Then
a dialogue began, and it was as if I was watching two actors on the stage. It
was between a character named **Grief** and one named **Life**.

*The experience began with **Grief** dominating and **Life** being dormant.*
*As time went on, **Life** opened up a little crack, but **Grief** said, "No, there*
is no place for you. This is too tragic."

    ***Life** said in a quiet voice, "I think I feel myself breathing again."*
    ***Grief** responded, "How could you? You've lost so much."*
    *As time went on and healers appeared, the dialogue got stronger. **Life***
said,
    *"I want to live and breathe." **Life** became passionate. "I want you to*
stop hurting."
    ***Grief** responded, "I will never stop hurting. The loss is too profound.*
You need to let me bleed."
    *And **Life** said, "You need to let me live."*
    *And so the conversation continued. **Life** believed that living would*
*never be possible with **Grief** around, and **Grief** was afraid that **Life***

would push away the need to honor the profound loss. **Life** *wanted to breathe and dance;* **Grief** *wanted to collapse and cry.*

Soon, **Life** *and* **Grief** *faced each other. They dropped the tug-of-war rope. Life said, "It is OK for you to cry and hurt for the rest of your life." Grief said, "It is OK for you to live."*

And so, they moved closer to each other. **Life** *knew it did not have to wait for* **Grief** *to go away in order to live.* **Grief** *knew that it was OK to hurt while* **Life** *was opening up.* **Grief** *and* **Life** *embraced and locked hands, now existing side by side.*

After hearing that dialogue I knew I couldn't sit and wait for grief to end in order to start living. Grief does not have to go away in the presence of abundant life and growth. When the two can exist side by side and it is not one or the other only, well, that is healing.

When I realized that I didn't have to be "healed" in order to start living, my journal entries started to be laced with hopeful movement, as a bud on a tree that has been dormant all winter, suddenly slowly opens into the light. The following journal entries indicate a moving out of the black, dark of night into more moments of light and spiritual movement.

THE FIFTEEN-FOOT HOLE

Periodically, I fall into the "fifteen-foot hole." It is dark. I crumble and break and fight. Then I breathe and start to ask questions. "What now?" Sometimes they are just questions, and other times, messages start to appear and guide me into the next leg of the journey. I climb out of the hole and take the next step, often feeling a warm stream of light.

I will never attempt to fill in that hole or bolt from it. It is necessary to drop into that dark place; it is the only chance I have of coming back up into the light. The depth of that hole represents the depth of love I have for Chloe and the pain of losing her. It propels me to grapple for the way, for the purpose and for the re-definition of myself. It becomes a place where the excavation of the soul continues.

COURAGE

I wear a charm around my neck that says "courage." Hope wears a ring with the same word. It takes so much of it to live each day. I realized something today: courage is not the absence of pain but the ability to recognize it and allow it to flow as profoundly as it needs to.

Every day seems to be an act of courage. Get up. Move forward. Just put one foot in front of the other. That is enough for now. In time, courage begets courage and grows strong and fierce. Fear begins to cower in its presence, and pain never needs to hide.

Courage is really trust. At times, I wanted to lie on the couch and stare at the ceiling all day or allow myself to fall into the deepest, darkest pit, and sometimes that was needed. But courage moves out into the black night, not knowing what is there or if it will lead you into any light at all. It just steps out because it trusts.

CONTROL

The hardest part about grief has been the loss of control. In the past I could always make a plan, create a map, and take steps to get where I wanted to go. But none of that mattered now; no planning or management or "ten steps" could get me what I wanted. Nothing would bring Chloe back. All control was lost. I had no say in it. I was a bystander, one that felt robbed of any voice in my life.

This powerful loss created fear inside me. What else was going to be "done" to me that I had no say in? Initially, I found that I could relieve this out-of-control feeling by doing something as simple as keeping order in my house. I desperately needed order. I couldn't allow piles to accumulate. Any order I could create cleared my mind and brought some peace. My mind was so full, trying to figure out how to function. There was a processor in my brain that was constantly running. I needed to keep other areas of my life from overwhelming me. I wore the same earrings and necklace every day. I stepped down from committees. I did only what needed to be done at work.

Eventually, I began to approach this loss of control differently. I had to allow my life to be out of control, to release the clutching, to trust deeply and begin to know that there is a divine order to my life, even in the midst of catastrophic events.

Courage isn't about being fearless—it's about feeling your fear and stepping through it.

GRATEFULNESS

I'm trying to find my way into gratefulness, even if it means going through the motions. I am grateful that I knew Chloe, that we are bonded in love forever, not just for twenty years. I'm grateful to have watched her grow into a funny, quirky, young-spirited girl, angered by injustice. I'm grateful for how she grew her soul and spirit and reflected on life and, in the end, found a way to respond to life internally and was able to follow her own beating heart.

Sometimes gratitude is difficult because it feels like pretending, somewhat robotic. The things I try to be grateful for really make me hurt. I look out at the gorgeous mountains that surrounded me, and I feel nothing. I can't see their beauty. I really want to say, "Thanks for nothing."

So what is this gratefulness thing, and does it work? I could spout off a list of things I was grateful for: a safe, warm home; the mountains surrounding me; my family, food, friends. But it felt like I was just reciting a child's dutiful, memorized prayer. Does grief need to exist beside gratitude? It feels like it is pushing grief out of the picture. How can gratitude and grief exist together? In "Where Does Gratitude Belong in Grief," Will Donnelly illustrates how we can use gratitude to turn sadness into something positive:

> We can literally change our relationship to life itself, turning baser emotions of anger, sadness, and bitterness, into something more powerful and positively creative. If all we can see is loss, then our spirits diminish and our lives shrink. We become grateful for what we can. When we accept gratitude as the major, dominant force in our lives, we radically neutralize the heavier forces of the ego that would have us live as victims of life and chance.

Maybe gratitude is a discipline, not a feeling; an activity that is engaged in to shift the brain from one state to the next. At this point in my journey, it doesn't come quite as easily as I would like. But what is working for me is, instead of manufacturing gratitude, I'm trying to be more in tune when sudden moments come that make me feel happy and loved. I stop, right at that moment, and say thank you.

A NEW TIME

I feel like I'm entering a new stage, a new time. I am immobilized on one level and functional on another. I think I am withdrawing a little more as I realize what a solo journey from tragedy to transformation this is. It is not for lack of loving family and friends; it is just the need to resolve my own loss. It is almost as though the reality of the magnitude of the loss is very sharp now. I am feeling things about Chloe's death that I could not feel in those first days. I can see it all, and with that comes a new wave of grief. And yet, I can feel moments of light and life.

I look the same on the outside, but my foundation is tilted. Inside, there is that stream of sorrow, trying to process where I'm at and who I am, what planet I've landed on, and how to accept and adapt to it. I find a greater weariness from the work I am doing. But I have hope and courage that I will find my way.

May I be at peace.

May my heart remain open.

May I know the beauty of my own true

nature.

May I be healed.

-JOAN BORYSENKO

PERSONAL VICTORY

Continued awareness of how my brain was functioning started leading me to some personal victories. This was one very significant triumph:

Today Herm left to go to Kansas for three days. When he left, I cried. It was an October day like October 24, 2010. I was here, Dillon was here; it was Sunday, and I needed to get groceries. The same scenario. My tears were not as much about missing Chloe or Herm as feeling this ripping kind of trauma racing through my body. A mild paralysis set in, and I decided I didn't have to get groceries. I sat and cried very deeply. I sat on the couch, hidden, frozen behind my laptop.

Later, a determination to conquer my fear came over me. I knew I had to do it. I walked out the door and out to the driveway. I stood in the spot where the world had come crashing down. I looked up into the sky. I just breathed over and over. This was a different time, a new time. It was a different sky, a different moment of the shining sun. I went to the car and drove away. I got groceries and came home. No one was waiting for me in my driveway to deliver the news. The sun was still shining. I still can't make that chocolate cake, as I had intended to do on the day Chloe died, but I am coming closer to understanding that buying that cake mix and making it will not cause history to repeat itself. I broke through my fear and experienced a personal victory.

Victories over traumatic events aren't completed in one action. They sometimes need to be re-lived or reworked many times, faced, and charged at, until they fall into the background and out of the driver's seat.

HELP FROM CHLOE

In the night, I had a dream. I was with some people somewhere, and all of a sudden, I looked up into the sky and a huge bird was taking shape in it. Then its tail feathers opened and spread out across the sky. I was awestruck. A girl was sitting beside me, gazing at the bird and she whispered Chloe's name like she knew it was her. We just stared at the sky. Then it would fade from sight, but still be there. Then it would appear again. The color of the bird was orange and brown with some yellow. I woke up and remembered the bird but wasn't sure of its meaning.

In the morning, Herm suggested we take the ATV and ride up to Caribou, a road that led to a place in the woods. I thought it would probably be good to get out in the sunshine and fresh air. We hadn't gotten very far and I laid my head on his back and started to cry.

When we got up to Caribou, I started thinking about the dream. I asked Chloe if there was any message there. She asked me how I felt when I saw the bird. I said I was awestruck by its enormous and beautiful presence. I felt completely wrapped up in it. She said her presence with me is that big. Sometimes I will feel it deeply, and sometimes I won't feel it at all, but she will still be there, just as when the bird faded from sight but did not leave. In that moment, I felt her, not just sitting beside me, but with me in the largest sense.

THE CENTER OF PAIN

After loss, we often hear, it is difficult to go to the places where tragedy occurred or places we shared with lost loved ones. Avoidance is supposed to alleviate the pain. I am the queen of avoidance when it comes to pain, and inclined to practice this. But surprisingly, living with all these dark clouds and shadows eventually led to more pain. I have found it far more helpful to bust right into the center of it like the sun breaking up a storm cloud. The heaviness dissipates, even if it brings tears. Going down the middle of each painful experience helps me get to the other side

An example of this was the day I decided to deal with Chloe's belongings. They were all sitting randomly in the basement bedroom. To go down there was like descending into hell. But I didn't want a dark room in my house, mainly because that darkness started to take up residence in my heart and body. This is, again, where courage comes in. Take a step and then another.

I opened the door and ventured in. I sat beside a box. On this day, I felt stronger, but holding each item still jabbed at my heart and stomach. I held her life in my hands, touching, feeling each one physically and emotionally, feeling Chloe, and remembering her. The more I worked, the greater need for order I had. I took out some things that were special and started displaying them on a shelf. I folded blankets, organized things into categories, and put boxes or bags in an orderly fashion around the room. I cried a little, but when I was done, I felt peace. I had touched everything. I knew what was there. The darkness had succumbed to the light.

I have come to see that pain holds a place for me. The deeper the pain, the greater the love, and the more I am propelled into my divine center. To fill that vacancy, that gap with something superficial would lessen the need to dive deep into my soul and expand into who I am fully meant to be.

Even though I painfully miss Chloe, I can be happy.

MESSAGES IN THE CANYON

Commuting down the canyon to work every day has some disadvantages, but the benefits far outweigh them. My time in silence had become a necessity. It is a safe place for grief to flow. In time, it became something else as well. I have been getting messages that have prompted me to ask questions and then receive more messages. I think the reason it happens in this space is that it is quiet and I am more receptive. There is no chance for interruption, and it has become a prayerful space for me. Initially, I hadn't planned on this being a place for spirit communication, but when I needed an answer or guidance, on most occasions, it came, though sometimes not immediately. It is not unusual to ask a question and then forget about it, only to get an answer a couple of days later. I can usually tell if my mind is drifting into my own thoughts or if it is a communication from Chloe or another spirit helper, mainly because I am often shocked or surprised at the answer. It is sometimes the opposite of the answer I had been entertaining, and often comes with details. The following are a few examples that have been significant to me.

1. THE ULTIMATE TEST

This morning as I was driving down the canyon, it was a snowy but sunny day. I felt like I was gliding in silence, and there was light around me. I felt peace creeping in. I wanted to push it away, and sit with my grief, but then I reminded myself to receive that peace that was coming to me. I started talking to Chloe. I told her I wanted her to be free and happy in her new life, but I still wanted communication. I was willing to do my part to try to understand how our relationship would change and what this new language was all about. Then it came . . . the message I heard was "This is the final test of letting your child go into her next stage of growth." I was somewhat shocked. This seemed like a reach. I stayed with the thought and soon started to feel that maybe, now, this is what love is.

It grieves me, but if Chloe is at her happiest moment, then I will bear that pain, giving her wings as I have always done in every other stage of her life.

2. EXISTENCE

I was driving up the canyon when I suddenly got hit with a message on existence. It came quite by surprise, as it was the furthest idea from my thoughts at the moment.

I sometimes feel like I exist almost solely for my children. On some level this is true, but on another level, I don't exist for them at all. I am here to fulfill my own purpose quite apart from them, and they have their own path. Although part of our growth may happen as a result of our relationship and we are all connected, we come together to help each other grow and move in our own given directions.

I want to be connected to Chloe. I want her and need her, but she exists to fulfill her divine purpose, and so do I. This was a revelation. My thinking had been totally the opposite. However, this idea became very liberating for me. It is a message I don't think I could have received until now. To know that Chloe does not exist to meet my needs and, on a spiritual level, I don't exist to meet hers. This releases us from each other, but the letting go actually creates a greater connection.

CLOSING THOUGHTS ON HEALING

Healing comes by stringing the lights together, one at a time. You won't feel like you're pursuing light; you won't even see it as light. It may all feel like darkness. But when you choose to meditate and clear your mind for five minutes, one light goes on in your soul, no matter how small. Sitting quietly with your loved one or in the presence of God allows a little more light to creep in. When you take a restorative yoga class, another one goes on. When you walk in the woods instead of staring at the ceiling, another goes on. You probably won't see it as light; you'll see it as an act of desperation, survival. When you touch a horse, read a book, climb a mountain, go fishing, learn about angel stones, you string lights together in your soul, even without your awareness. In between the lights, there may be darkness. Hold it, weep, feel it. But if you keep stepping out of the darkness, soon the collective light starts shining brighter, and you feel it; you see it, and you move from surviving to thriving.

My poem for a new time:

I AM
    I am
    sad
    lost
    aching
    shattered
    crushed
    despondent
    courageous
    strong
    expanded
    loving
    compassionate
    living
    hoping

    All of this…I am.

CHAPTER 8

Reflection, Meditation and Practice

FOR ME, HEALING HAPPENED BOTH internally and externally. Practices such as yoga, meditation and writing helped me to turn inward, reflecting on my experience and the feelings I was bringing to it. Movement was also crucial—not just physical movement, such as dancing or riding horses, but trying new things, moving to a new location and finding new social groups. In this section I share practices and actions that I engaged in to keep myself healthy and on a healing path. Some of them were taken from my journal with added reflections about what I learned from that experience. It did not always come natural to take "action" on this journey. I was quite content, at times, to stare at the ceiling or hide behind my computer. But action brought life, and feeling life again brought joy and so I made efforts to step out and move in new directions.

Healing is multidimensional. It takes science to provide us with basic facts about what has happened and continues to happen. It requires work within the physical body to release what our mind cannot. Our "Spirit Tribe" including God, angels and guides help in ways that we may not expect or understand. Everything in this chapter falls into one of those categories, and I have had a need for them all simultaneously on this intricate path.

MEDITATION

Although I was familiar with prayer, I had never had much patience for meditation. To clear my mind and sit in stillness was a monumental task for my busy mind. Still, I decided that now was the time to give it some attention and effort and bring it into my life.

The intent of meditation is to clear and still the mind, just breathing in the present moment, suspending the endless chatter that often consumes our days. Prayer is different. In prayer, one is generally turning their attention toward God, asking for help, giving thanks or just talking. I found that I needed them both, only the "talking to God" part took a while. I have found meditation beneficial in helping me to relax, ease my fears and anxieties and pull all my fragments into one centered place. Some days I can only sit still for five minutes. On other days the time flies and I am amazed that I have been able to sit so long.

I didn't follow a prescribed method or technique to meditate. I just started by breathing. Different types of beaded bracelets helped me focus and stay positive. One was a set of amethyst beads with a silver labyrinth charm, another was a circle of garnets with a silver heart charm, and the last was a string of Chloe's own orange and brown beads. As I touched each one, I took a breath or said a phrase. The recitation I used the most was from Julian of Norwich, who is regarded as an important Christian mystic: "All shall be well, and all shall be well, and all manner of thing shall be well."

As meditation became more of a regular practice, I realized it had other benefits for me, personally. I became aware of what I was really feeling and was able to bring sadness and heartbreak to the surface. There was no pushing it down and away. This often brought tears but they were needed. Also, as I cleared my mind of clutter I was better able to listen and communicate with Chloe. I learned that if I was going to continue to meet her and hear from her this would need to become a discipline and regular practice.

YOGA

I had never attempted one contorted yoga pose in my life. But now I needed it. I needed to breathe; I needed to feel the ache working from the inside of my body to the outside. I found it especially helpful to go through this routine on my deck. There was an added sensory dimension in feeling the breeze and breathing the pure air. There were always birds to keep me company and the occasional visits of butterflies and hummingbirds. Sometimes I just went through the poses with my eyes closed, and that in itself was a meditation. It often helped the pain to surface, but other times, I was perfectly peaceful.

On one particular day, I felt like I wanted to spend some time alone. I went upstairs and sat on the floor on my yoga mat. I lit a candle and put Chloe's pictures around me. I talked to her, I loved her. Then I meditated for a while. Clearing my mind and emotions started to bring me a sense of peace. I did my yoga in attempt to release grief from my body, not thinking or hurting, just focused on each movement. At the end, I felt more grounded and peaceful.

Coming to my mat became a kind of refuge. It was a meditation space, a place to talk to Chloe, to check in with myself and to clear my mind and heart of any heaviness. I was gaining physical strength and becoming more aware of who I was. Every ache my body and soul held was left in that space.

WRITING

I started journaling two months after losing Chloe. It was a way for me to be totally true to myself, my experience, and my timeline. I held back nothing. It was my sanctuary. I chose my own language and followed no guidelines. This was mine, all mine, and all that was inside me freely flowed.

When dreams, messages, and contact started to come, I didn't want to let them slip away. I wanted to remember every image, sound, and feeling. As I read back over those entries, some of them have opened up new meanings that I was not capable of seeing in my initial raw state of grieving.

Writing held more of a purpose than just capturing those moments. The process itself is like talking to a close friend, without the need to monitor words or feelings. It has been kind of like my "heart-flow" or a less emotional form of crying. It all comes out onto the paper and I no longer need to hold it inside. The beauty of journaling is that you make up the rules. You can write in sentences or phrases, in lines or circles. Sometimes I wrote in pictures or symbols. There is no judgment or value placed on your thoughts or how you lay them on the paper. It is your own "Secret Garden."

READING

I have never read so much in my entire life. I began with books about parents who had lost children and then people who had experienced other losses. Reading about parents who had stayed connected with their children piqued my interest in what could be learned from Near Death Experiences, Spirit Activity and Communication, Heaven, Angels and Mediums. I read everything with curiosity and reflection on my own shifting belief system. Spirit connection was the newest idea to me. I needed answers for what I was experiencing. It wasn't that I didn't believe in spirit connection, I just never had a reason to learn about it. I found a lot of myths and fears being dispelled.

In addition to the reading I was doing as I tried to complete my Master's Program in Information Learning Technologies, I also read books about brain theory, grief, trauma, and horses, not to mention the numerous articles read online encompassing all these subjects and more. I found it necessary to also throw in a few novels and kids' books to lighten things up.

I was not very eager to reclaim my old social life and reading became a kind of bridge to the world out there and the experience I was going through. It was easier to relate to an author who shared my experience than to engage in empty conversations at social events.

SURVIVE OR THRIVE

It seems that how you survive tragedy depends largely on who you were before it occurred, your belief system, your commitment to growth, whether you were prone to depression, had a positive or dismal outlook on life, and so on. I think that I have had things that have benefited me and will bring me through this, and probably some patterns that aren't serving me well.

I have always loved life and enjoyed pursuing dreams and aspirations, working at not being afraid of life but engaging it. I am always on an endless journey for truth and true spirituality, so in a sense, it was no surprise that I found myself propelled into that journey on a deeper level in the face of loss. It required that I develop new practices, a broader perspective, and suspend any disbelief I might have had about life and death in order not to block any messages that might be trying to get through to me. I knew it would be impossible to do this work in a noisy world which is one of the reasons I chose not to quickly return to work but to surround myself with the quietness of nature.

I worked on developing my senses and began adding intuition to this effort. The ones I found myself gravitating toward are what I called "spiritual senses"—those needed to understand life on a spiritual level while combining them with physical and scientific knowledge.

I developed a morning mantra that I recited on my way to work:

Open my eyes that I might see;
Open my ears to hear.
Open my mind to understanding;
Open my intuition to knowing, believing,
and trusting.
Open my heart to love and to be loved.

Spiritual Vortexes

There are two main definitions for vortexes. On one hand, there's a simple and scientific definition. In the world of hard facts and proof, a vortex is defined as a swirling mass of substance such as air, water, or fire. Examples of these vortexes could be cited as tornadoes, whirlpools, and volcanoes. These vortexes are based on fact and science. But since the early 1920s, another definition of vortex has emerged into the surface of consciousness.

> *"Spiritual vortexes are said to be cross points between energy*
> *fields in the earth's grid system, or intersecting ley lines. Where*
> *the ley lines intersect, in certain areas, the result is said to be a*
> *"hot spot" of energy that can produce a wide range of effects along*
> *the lines of spiritual healing and psychic enhancement."*

—WENDI FRIEND

There are many spiritual vortexes in nature where there is greater receptivity to spirit communication and healing. Nature is multisensory to the heart, mind and spirit. Grief requires more time next to the earth. The quietness found there also allows for greater connection and cleansing of the mind and emotions.

For me, no matter how scientific or spiritual an idea is, if I can't have a true experience with it, it means nothing. But in the case of vortexes, I have often felt a shift in my energy and spirit, a sense of leaving the place where I'm sitting and yet remaining connected to it. I have had three experiences with spiritual vortexes that I can remember. One came through a deep feeling, a frozen moment in time:

I stood in the pasture, and the snow was lightly falling. It was dancing on my face with gentle strokes. Chloe felt so close, as if our worlds were melding. Life just opened up, and everything was breathing again. Everywhere I looked, I saw her, felt her. I felt myself. In the old buildings she would love to explore, the trails with their mysteries and treasures, the barn, and the animals. I wondered why we didn't get to share this in life on the ranch. Will we be better able to share it now?

The other two experiences were a combination of what I was feeling and seeing. Both happened after brief meditations, and both happened in the woods. The first was in my place near the three trees.

I went to my place between three trees and began breathing softly. I closed my eyes and cleared my mind and talked to Chloe. The warm air held the sweetness of the coniferous trees that surrounded me. I felt the softness of the earth under my blanket. My heart was calm and peaceful. There was something passing from myself to Chloe and back again. Just a shared, silent moment. I realized how rare it is to experience this in my earthly relationships because they are full of busyness and noise. I am learning that it is enough just to "be," and it is actually quite beautiful. I opened my eyes, and I saw something in front of me that was like transparent waves. The best way I can describe it is to compare it to exhaust fumes you might see coming out of a car, but there was a clarity to them and a pattern. They were not fast and jerky but they just hung there in space, making subtle movements. But they did not linger, and quickly dissipated. There was a feeling inside me in that moment of utter awe, and at the same time mystery. I don't intend to explain what happened there or even understand it. I do feel like I was brought to some kind of intersection of the earthly and spiritual plane.

The second time this happened, I was in the woods at our new house. It was Chloe's birthday, and I had taken the day off of work just to spend some quiet time with her.

The air was warm and the sun was shining as I headed out the door to the woods. Our house is nestled in a small valley flanked on each side by the forest. I had not done much exploring yet since we had only lived here a year. I chose to go to the east and see what I could find. I climbed up a small incline and found a clearing with a few trees where the sun was shining down on the ground. I put my jacket down and began listening to some music on my phone. I had no real agenda other than to check in with Chloe and talk to her about her birthday and other things. It was also a time for me to be alone and enjoy the beauty of nature. I closed my eyes and tried to feel what was around me, to listen carefully to the subtle sounds and to breathe. I cleared my thoughts and tried to get out of my head and into my heart. When I opened my eyes, I saw it. This time it was to the right of me, those waves. If I had to describe a color, I would say silver-blue, but not solid. More like a spiral. It happened very quickly, and when I shifted from my meditative state to my intellect and tried to understand it, it disappeared.

BECOMING A WARRIOR

According to Guy Finley in his article *"Ten Traits of the True Spiritual Warrior,"* a warrior never postpones a battle that must be engaged. The true spiritual warrior is never afraid to look at what he doesn't want to see. He knows that the path of spiritual liberation he has chosen must lead him to one encounter after another with conditions that always seem greater than he is.

I could not describe my life any better than this. My natural inclination and response in the face of fear and loss is to live in a state of paralysis and collapse—to cease to move and even to breathe. But that state will only contribute to my own death. And so every day I put one foot forward, moving straight through the pain to the other side where I know there will be light. Does this movement speak to my strength and power? No, it is a movement of courage which, on some days, is mighty and on other days totally dormant.

The warrior image has been life-changing for me. Most of my life I have been in pursuit of happiness, fighting to get away from any pain or discomfort when it came my way. I never saw life challenges as holding any purpose. There was nothing to be gained from them and if I just ran or hid from them then I could get on to a more pleasant existence. But I have had no choice. Losing Chloe wasn't something I could ignore. The only chance at life now was to turn and face my fear and all of the other demons that wanted to paralyze me. The visual of seeing myself as a brave warrior who steps into each day without fear of loss or being consumed by sadness has helped me get out of bed and conquer the tasks and emotions of each day.

HORSES

One afternoon as I was wrapping up my day, a colleague and good friend popped her head into my classroom and simply said, "I'm going to walk with you on this journey." I will probably never forget those words, as it had only been a short time after losing Chloe, and knowing how to approach or support a grieving person can be tricky. I didn't always even know what I needed. But Lori took a chance. We began talking and she told me about the loss of her mother, and how it propelled her into horses. She offered herself as a resource to me as I pursued an equine therapist and later purchased my two horses. One day she came to me with a bag of books about horses. Most of them were about a horse's ability to connect with humans in a rather spiritual way. I became intrigued with these large beings who were, maybe, more than just beautiful. Lori invited me to the ranch where she boarded her horses. As I drove into the lane and looked to the right, I saw an expansive pasture with the graceful bodies of more than twenty horses wandering aimlessly across it. Bodies brushing each other, tails swishing, they were both wild and gentle all at the same time. I gazed at their muscular structure and wondered how something with so much power could connect with me at a heart level. We entered the pasture. I was not afraid, but happy and calm just being around them. We started walking into the field and they came and surrounded us. Maybe they were just curious or thought we were part of the herd, but I felt a peaceful, calm filling me up. I left happy and motivated to enter the equine world.

Therapeutic riding centers are increasing in droves. But why? Horses are rather majestic and magical, but how do they actually help in the healing journey? I had no idea when I made the step to ride, why or how they could help me.

One of my favorite movies is *The Horse Boy*. It is an account of how a child with autism improves immeasurably in his experiences with horses. Activities that combine both rhythm and balance such as horseback riding help stabilize a disordered sensory system. I became curious about the research done on horses and humans. Studies have shown that just being around horses changes human brain-wave patterns, however, I felt that research was irrelevant if I wasn't having an experience that matched it. The real research was going to be my own that I would gather as I began working with an equine therapist and then as I moved into horse ownership.

I took my riding lesson once a week for an hour. No matter what emotional state I came to the stable in, when I was done I always felt peaceful and happy. At times it was more strategically focused on grief work, other times it was riding technique and grooming. Riding required me to be present in every moment with the horse. I had to constantly be aware of my body and the message it was sending to the horse. Every lesson began with breathing as I circled the arena. When my body was ready, the lesson could begin.

Journey Ride

One day, I came to my lesson feeling my train-wrecked heart was about to explode, and yet, not even acknowledging it to myself. I knew I couldn't do the physical and mental work of riding today. I lacked focus, and my heart ached. My trainer said just to come, and we would do a journey ride.

We stood outside the stall. She asked me how I was. I told her of my fatigue, lack of focus, and vacancy. I didn't really feel any tears, although I did feel a pressure in my stomach like I was holding on to something. We kept talking, and the tears started to come. She handed me the halter and told me to go in and be with the horse for as long as I needed. I went in and stood beside him. I put my arms around his neck and started to sob. Everything just came rolling out. I put the halter on, and we led him over to get him ready. As I groomed him, we talked some more. We went to the arena. I was asked to close my eyes and travel up my body and observe anything I felt. When we were done, she asked me what I had observed. I said I could feel some shakiness in my legs and tightness in my stomach and heart. She said we didn't need to change that, only to observe. Before I got on the horse, she asked me what my intent was. I said it was to feel the horse, to be with Chloe, and to become more centered and peaceful.

She asked me who I wanted with me on the ride. I said, "Chloe." She asked me where I wanted Chloe to be. I said, "Riding with me, sitting behind me." She tied up the reins and took the lead rope and began to lead the horse all around the arena. I closed my eyes. I had no plan. I began to just feel the horse's body and rhythm. This is the dialogue between myself and Chloe that came:

Me: Chloe, it is OK for you to be who you are now, and I can be who I am, and we can still be together. Put your arms around me, lay your head on my back. I release you from needing to be here in your physical form. You can be in the place where you are. We can be together in our own forms.

Silence.

My trainer stopped somewhat suddenly. I opened my eyes, and she asked, "What just happened?" I told her that I had found a way into releasing Chloe. She told me that at that moment, the horse had made a gesture and sound with its mouth that is a sign of release and relaxation.

We continued on.

I breathed my familiar meditation mantra: "All will be well, all will be well, and all manner of things will be well." Repeat.

Silence.

Me: [in silent meditation] I am with you, and you are with me." Repeat... repeat...repeat.

Silence.

Me: [in silent meditation] I give myself to this time. I give myself to this sorrow. I give myself to this grief and this pain. Repeat.

She stopped the horse to check in with me. I opened my eyes. It had been a near miraculous time. I was relaxed, all tension was gone. I could feel myself again. I felt grounded and all those fragments seemed to come back together. I felt together again, centered.

The next morning, I woke up wide awake, it took no effort to get out of bed. I felt good, with a strong, positive energy. Even though there is a sorrowful place inside me, I felt more alive.

My experiences with the positive effect of horses continued outside the arena as well. I found that trauma caused me to freeze, physically and emotionally. There was nothing rational about it; I was just afraid. As I started to ride horses, it brought movement into my life. Sometimes when I was lying down at night, trying to turn off my scattered brain, I would go into an imaginary canter, feeling the gentle, smooth up-and-down movements of the horse, and I was moving again, I relaxed and became unafraid.

I don't know if I'll ever be a good rider, but after learning how to feel the horse under my body during the canter, I started to realize the importance of movement. When I was not with the horses, the canter continued to help me stay in a place of calm steadiness. I would close my eyes and feel the movement lifting me up and then floating back down in regular rhythm.

Equine therapy helped me to see the benefits that horses had for me. Within a couple years after losing Chloe, our family had moved onto a ranch, a place that brought healing moments, nature, wild animals, Aspen trees, working with the earth . . . and with horses. I'm pretty sure we made the decision to get our two horses, Ace and Tahoe, before we were adequately prepared. I underestimated how the horses would react to their new surroundings and how I would react to their apprehension. I became afraid on every level.

We picked up the horses in two different locations, and the owners helped load them into our trailer, our first time ever hauling horses. When we arrived home, it was getting dark. We got the horses out one at a time in an awkward, uncertain fashion. I could feel immediately that their energy was larger and stronger than it had been with their previous owners. Their eyes harbored fear and anxiety. There was nothing smooth about this first experience. The horses moved back and forth, and their gait was quick and strong. We managed to get them each in separate stalls for the night.

What happened in the days that followed required me to examine fear on what felt like a global level. I was afraid to go near the horses and stepped into the barn cautiously. They were not relaxed, they seemed twice as large as I remembered and I was afraid of getting hurt. The more my fear grew, the stronger and more agitated they became. It was becoming a vicious cycle. One day, as I was preparing to go to the barn, I stopped and sat down on the warped, wooden steps leading to the barn. I felt as if I had suddenly slammed into a brick wall and saw my fear for the giant it had become. I whispered to myself, you can't go into the barn afraid anymore. I took a few deep breaths and walked slowly toward the stalls. I stood quietly and talked to the horses and breathed some more. I was now making a conscious decision to trust them and myself. The horses started to relax and slow down, but the experience had taken me to a larger level of awareness. It wasn't just about the horses. I realized that when I perceive something to be bigger than me, whether it is a project, activity, or personality, I become afraid. I began to think about all the things I was actually afraid of. I then proceeded to think about different reactions I could have to any type of fear. Breathe, slow down, trust, and act unafraid.

The next lesson I learned is that there is no way for horses to lie. They are completely authentic and transparent. It is impossible for them to pretend, and so they become confused when our actions are not congruent with what we are feeling inside. In this way, they can help us examine what is true of our experience, even if we are not totally aware of it in the moment. They mirror what they sense in us. Fear was my first experience with this. Authenticity was my second.

As people began visiting the ranch, they wanted to interact with the horses. Some had been around horses: maybe they had ridden, or maybe they just liked them. Many wanted to ride. This made me anxious, as I felt responsible for these large animals as well as the people. I was only beginning to know the horses and considered myself a novice. I had successfully worked with them on the ground. They knew what I wanted and followed my intent and commands. They would easily back up, walk left, walk right, turn in a circle, trot, and canter. One evening, a group of people were visiting our house, and a young man who loved horses wanted to work with them. I decided some ground work would be OK. I brought Tahoe into the arena. The young man and a few others were watching me. I gave him the first command to back up. Not only would he not back up, but he started pushing his weight around in side-to-side motions. He was becoming anxious, and I could see our exercise was going nowhere. I was not only a little embarrassed; I was baffled.

Later that evening, I sat, feeling into that whole experience. I realized that I had become someone that Tahoe didn't recognize. People had been watching, and I had turned into a "performer." I had discarded authenticity for the appearance of being an accomplished "horsewoman." Fail. This lesson translated into my life as I started becoming aware of who I am when people are watching and who I am alone. I realized that I sometimes "stage" myself out of fear that I will receive less love or approval without performing at a certain level. I have now come to frequently ask myself this question: does what's on the inside match with what's on the outside? Who we are and what we feel on the inside should drive our actions on the outside.

Thus far in my research about the connection between human and horse I have found that, quite simply, horses are intuitive, nonjudgmental, and offer unconditional love. Merely touching their bodies and being next to them is enough. Over time, I learned about the benefits of movement and how it soothed my nervous system. Horses mirror my heart and require me to be present in every moment. They led me to the truth that was aching in my heart, whether it was sadness, loneliness or feeling lost. I didn't have to keep it hidden, I only had to acknowledge it. They let me be wherever I am in life, and they're OK when I'm weak and crying or abundantly joyful. I feel the horses propelling me forward, forcing me to listen, watch, and communicate more intently.

DANCING

When I lost Chloe, I quit dancing. I have been in and out of dance classes since I was twenty-three. In the third year, I received an e-mail about a dance show that would be happening on the fourth anniversary: October 24th. I felt something move inside me, but I was afraid and also excited to dance on that day. Could I do it? Would I cry or become weak? Would I forget the routine? I couldn't predict my reaction to this day, but still I moved toward that goal. I began in January. It was uncomfortable at first, walking into a community that I did not yet belong to. I felt unseen. I had no stamina and had to make myself go to class. Focus was a challenge. It required so much mental concentration and, at times, I would just miss it all or stare off into space. But I kept going, taking baby steps toward that goal.

By October, the rehearsal schedule, became so rigorous while trying to also work full time, that I was more focused on surviving than giving attention to my emotional state or to the events of that anniversary. When the weekend of the performance arrived, I knew I was just going to dance. I had a purpose for being there. I didn't allow death to keep me from life. Even if I never danced again, this action gave me a renewed strength and confidence in my ability to overcome my fear and weakness. I took my imperfect body to the dance floor. The music began. I took a breath, and I danced.

Shortly after my return to dance, I found Movement Mass. It was quite different from the jazz and ballet classes I took during the week. This was a more meditative dance, done to various genres of music and varied rhythms throughout the session. It opened with a prayerful moment as the participants gathered in a circle. The music started slowly and increased in pace with people moving in their own style or even not moving at all, but only listening. There were no steps to follow, no choreography to learn. The music and dance build up to what might appear as chaos to an onlooker. The first time I went, I moved only slightly at the beginning. The tears found me, and I let them come. Every mass was different for me—sometimes joyful, sometimes feeling Chloe's presence deeply, and I even found my way to chaos. As I began moving through all of the rhythms, I felt my body releasing all of my emotional, physical, and spiritual contents, like the wringing out of a wet washcloth...a grief cleansing. Dance, in any form, pulls together the mind, body and spirit.

Emotional Freedom Tapping (EFT)

After my session with Cheryl to contact Chloe, I decided it would be beneficial for me to continue seeing her as my therapist. I had a sense that this was a place that I could find continued healing and renew my life purpose in the context of Chloe's death. In addition to talking and exploring my emotions and experiences, we also worked at the physical, cellular level to release the trauma using EFT.

"Conventional medicine, at its foundation, focuses on the
biochemistry of cells, tissue, and organs. Energy Medicine, at its
foundation, focuses on the energy fields of the body that organize

and control the growth and repair of cells, tissue, and organs. Changing impaired energy patterns may be the most efficient, least invasive way to improve the vitality of organs, cells, and psyche."

—DAVID FEINSTEIN, PH.D.

This was new to me but I knew that working with the body was as important as working with my emotions. I was willing to try anything that would keep my body healthy. The technique seemed so simple. Massaging, twisting or connecting specific energy points, tracing or swirling the hand over the skin, tapping around my head, sides, holding a position—sometimes it felt like I was just holding myself. It was a simple practice and one I could do at home as part of my meditations or as a stand-alone practice. As certain points on the body are tapped a phrase is said which acknowledges the problem and expresses acceptance for yourself in spite of it. It doesn't really seem like you're doing anything, but when you compare your body before and after the practice, you can feel that there has been an emotional shift.

Donna Eden, an Energy Medicine Practitioner and captivating teacher puts it in practical terms:

"Energy is your body's magic! It is your life force. You keep it healthy and it keeps you healthy. If you are sick or sad, shifting your energies feels good. When you care for these invisible energies, it makes your heart sing and your cells happy!"

Intuitive Healers

My reading and conversations with friends and intuitive therapists helped me to understand that there is another way to approach life and death. In addition to my mind and its cognitive way of processing, I could develop a keener intuition and gain information and communication with Chloe.

After exhaustive reading on mediums, intuitive healers and spirit communication, I finally decided to find someone who might be able to contact

Chloe. I explored several websites and settled on a woman who works by herself in her home. We exchanged a few emails and I made the appointment. As the day approached I felt nervous about what I might experience. I was full of anticipation but also afraid of the unknown. Would it be real? Maybe she had just spent the day Googling Chloe and brushed up on information that was already available. She had only asked for Chloe's first name and wanted no more information. I arrived at her house located in a peaceful, wooded area and tentatively approached the door. A short, friendly woman met me with a welcoming warmth which soon put me at ease. I stepped in and looked around at the cozy, quaint features of the room. I sat down on a comfortable chair. I was totally out of my element, and curious at the same time. She explained how it worked: She did not want to me to offer any information, only verify the messages she was getting. She told me she had been talking to Chloe earlier in the day, but never knew how or if a spirit will choose to come through. In the back of my mind I still kind of expected information she might have found in one of the news articles, but she offered none of that. What she did begin with was telling me the essence of who Chloe was, something only a parent, sibling or close friend would know. She told me that she enjoyed nature and she could easily be alone and that she liked to sing. Here are a few excerpts from the conversation.

Alina: She feels quiet and introspective, but it wasn't that she didn't like to communicate with people, with people she was close to she was very good at communicating, but she wasn't an overly vivacious, out-there person. It wasn't that she was shy—she didn't share herself with everyone casually. Still waters run deep. She was quiet, but the people who knew her knew she was always thinking. She was very bright.

The feeling I was getting is that she went away to college. She had so many loves and so many abilities that she had a hard time figuring out what direction to channel it. When she went to college I think she hoped it would help her figure out a direction to go, but she just felt like it wasn't speaking to her. It wasn't helping her to figure out a direction. I think she just felt like there was a lot more meaning to everything. She was good at school and she saw the purpose in it, but it was just kind of vapid, like there was just so much more. She wanted to get on with things. I think it might have been a spiritual knowing that her time was limited. She needed to get busy. She didn't want to waste years in school.

She has a very tender heart and tender spirit. She really felt for people, people who were in need and she felt like she needed to be doing something and sitting in school felt like a waste of time when she knew she could go and be of use to people and be of service, and I think she felt like in doing that, that things would start falling into place, that the right opportunities would come up and she would be led to the next place.

She wanted you to know that, in the accident, she didn't feel anything. She wants you to know she didn't suffer. A lot of times what happens is it's like they're plucked from their body before it ever even happens. It's like an angel just takes them so they don't experience any traumatic feelings. She's just kind of showing me, she feels bad how hard that was for you guys. She was watching you find out, and the struggle and the shock, and all that.

Alina: The reading that you have now and the reading you would have in a year are different because they will have jobs. It's weird because they talk about heaven as a real tangible place. They see things, they do things, they feel things, they see, smell, taste. It's not a material existence like our world, which is motivated by material things. But it is a real, tangible place.

Alina: I'm trying to clarify with her if she knows yet what she's going to do . . . it's probably too soon. Was part of the work she was doing in Alamosa; did it have anything to do with kids? Because I feel like . . . was it abused or mistreated kids? I feel it bothered her, the innocent children being victimized. So I think that's probably one of her passions. I feel like that's the direction she's going. She's saying that she can do a lot more from the other side than she can do here. She can be in so many different places and help so many more people without the restrictions that we have here. She can be with the children during their trauma.

Alina: Was her dog a boy dog? Does he have an RS sound in his name? Is his name Roscoe? (Chloe's dog's name was Oscar. During the reading Alina was holding her dog on her lap. Her dog's name was Chloe. She held her dog because animals can help a spirit come through).

Alina: She just wants you to know that she loves you and she's with you and that she's OK. She knows how hard it is for you and how much you miss her. She feels that. She feels you talking to her. Do you ever write to her? She wants you to know that she knows all that and she sees it. She just wants you to carry on and do what you're meant to do with your life. She's going to wait for you; you'll see each other again. She doesn't want this to be something that stops you or holds you back. The main thing that Chloe wants is for this to not be wasted.

Cindy: I have had many dreams of Chloe coming to me and giving me messages and answering questions. Is that really her?

Alina: Dreams—yes, that is her. To hear a spirit is a very subtle quiet thing. Grief is noisy. Your loved one is a wind chime and your grief is a neighbor shooting off fireworks. You have to quiet the pain and grief in order to hear them. The advantage you have is that you've drawn on that spiritual core to help quiet yourself. You're lucky to be having those experiences. Try to stay in a positive place. Don't beat yourself up if you have a bad day or stage; just let yourself move through it. But if you do that, you will continue to feel her presence in your life more and more and more. Funneling your grief in a positive direction will help you to be able to feel her.

One of the things she was just coming through with is that she really wants you to help people with grief. It wasn't Chloe's physical body you loved, it was her spirit. In some ways you may be closer now than you ever were. Once you realize that they're not gone, you can allow it to evolve to a whole new level. You are dealing with grief so beautifully and so gracefully.

Cindy: Can spirits manifest themselves into animals?

Alina: Yes, and they do it a lot, you'll notice it in butterflies. She's got a very clear energy and a very clear purpose, very driven. She just has this love about her. Not only is she going to send those validations, but you're *going to see them. You have so much to teach and so much to share that I hope you do something with that.*

Alina: It makes me emotional listening to you because of the place that you've gotten to with your grief. It's all I wish for people.

I only saw Alina once, as she was a little far from where I lived, but being with her as she contacted Chloe was like getting one more text, one more phone call. When I made the appointment with her Herm had asked if he could go along, but this was something I needed to do alone. When he asked if he could drive me, I said that would be fine. He waited in the truck. As he sat there a herd of elk came and gathered around him. A spiritual presence seemed to be everywhere that day.

Several weeks later a friend gave me a phone number of another medium, but I didn't pursue it. I had scratched the number down and thrown it somewhere in my house. I wasn't quite ready to meet her. I needed to keep the experience with Alina in my heart for a while. Over the next year that paper with her number kept falling out in front of me. I would just pick it up and put it back in another pile or drawer. I never threw it away, but I didn't want to act on it either. One day I was ready to leave for work and I went out to my car. Just as I was ready to open the door, I looked down and there was the small piece of paper with the phone number laying on the pavement. I picked it up and knew that now was the time to call. I searched for her website to learn a little more about her. Cheryl Breault, LPC, a therapist, intuitive healer and educator. She had a broad range of experience, mediumship being only a part of her work. I made an appointment to have Chloe contacted once again. I wasn't as nervous now, but more excited. It was over a year later. I was hoping she would come again.

This time, I did not have to travel far, as Cheryl was located in the same town I worked in. I walked up the sidewalk to her office, a beautiful old house which she shared with several other therapist-type people. She opened the door and I relaxed at once, being surrounded with her immediate love and warmth.

The room was comfortable and inviting. A sofa with some pillows, plants, a few pictures, a couple lamps and a stuffed chair that sat across from the sofa. She directed me to the sofa and began describing how the process would work. It is never a given that a spirit will come through as they have choices too. Cheryl said she didn't know if Chloe would come through today. The session began with a prayer, which was more of a reading, but very beautiful. When it was done, I looked up and saw that there were tears in Cheryl's eyes. She said, "She loves you so much and she is so excited to see you." I got chills and felt so much joy, like I've never experienced. I don't think I've ever felt that kind of bliss, even before Chloe died.

Cheryl continued, "The two of you don't need me, you're already connected." This was a powerful confirmation that what I had been experiencing was real. I appreciated this immensely, but I asked her to go on.

The flavor of this session was loving, lighthearted and fun. Chloe was first sitting up on the back of the sofa and then in another part of the room. At one point she was telling me that there was a picture in our house of her that she really liked. The frame had some blue and purple and silver, it was somewhat ornate. I told Cheryl I couldn't recollect any picture or frame in our house that fit that description so we moved on. This reading had such a different flavor than the first one. When I first met with Alina, Chloe had been gone only 4 months. It was filled with the assurance that she was OK and that she was still with us and loved us. Over a year later, my session with Cheryl revealed how happy she was and also still connected. It wasn't some angelic being who came through. It was Chloe and her funny, quirky personality, as alive as ever. I left Cheryl's office full of hope and happiness.

Later that week, I was sitting in my living room and I glanced up at the fireplace mantel. There it was, the picture frame with Chloe's picture, the one she had been trying to explain in our session. It was blue and purple with silver sequins, curves and scallops and shiny flowers. Yes, you could describe it as "ornate" but I had always thought of it as "gaudy." Now I loved it all the more.

Heaven and Eternal Connection

I'm realizing that my concept of heaven or the "afterlife" has been so limited and narrow. I had no idea the wealth of knowledge that is available from so many earthly and spiritual beings. Even though I don't think we can ever receive the full picture of what awaits us, this has all been very intriguing to me. While I have never had a reason to dig up answers about heaven, I realized that there are many people around me who read, study, and contact those who have crossed over in order to gain new information. Receiving an awareness from Chloe was the most meaningful of those experiences. Just by asking, I saw her new place of residence in a multisensory dream. Of all the books I have read, conversations I have had, and my own contact from Chloe, I am gaining a greater sense of this journey and our purpose here in the grand scheme of things. We are all working at spiritual growth consciously and sometimes unconsciously as well.

Through the many individuals who have had near-death experiences and mediums who have received messages from spirits and through advancements in technology, we now have a greater wealth of information about heaven (or whatever name you would like to give it). While "rest in peace" may, in some way, apply to the physical body, it in no way applies to our loved ones' activities in heaven. Peace, yes, but they are not resting. They are very busy with learning and carrying out their own work.

I have learned about Chloe's life in spirit in a number of ways. The two different mediums in different parts of the state had the same message. She would be working to help kids facing challenging circumstances. I also received this message in a dream about Cabbage Patch Kids. I initially thought, *how cute*, until the nudging and prompting confirmed her work with kids. I was driving to work and thinking about the dream and it didn't seem like much, but then I thought more about it: helping children—"cabbage-patch" kids are homeless kids without families. It all started coming together. Her work now was with kids in challenging life situations.

It is no surprise that Chloe's sister, Hope, found herself working in a wilderness therapy program with kids coming with their own life challenges. One experience illuminated Chloe's presence with her in this work. When Chloe was about 12 years old we were on a family vacation. Chloe was riding in the front passenger seat and suddenly declared, "You know, dad, there's really only one road, because they're all connected." We laughed at her "insight" and used that phrase on many trips. It was a family joke that we never shared with anyone. After Chloe died and Hope was working in the woods one day, she was walking with one of the students alone on a mountain path. Suddenly he said, "You know Hope, there's really only one road." Hope immediately new the significance of those words: Chloe was very close.

Learning and education continue in heaven as work is done to develop spiritual passions. In a morning meditation, I asked Chloe to show me what she is working on or learning. I saw her in some type of large, white building with her guitar. This is not surprising, as music was her meditation, her joy. She has already begun working with Herm. One day as he sat outside on the porch, I could hear his guitar stop and start, stringing a melody together. I couldn't hear the words, just bits and pieces of a tune. It was just a background hum. A few days later, he gave me the lyrics to the completed song. A different sensation came over me. As my eyes fell on the last word, I looked up and said, "This is not your song." I know his writing, and I have, only recently, become aware of Chloe's as I have read her writing and listened to the songs she left on Herm's laptop.

Herm responded, "I know. It's our song."

Healing, by my definition, has come through the continued connection and working relationship with Chloe. It is not easy, by any means. It takes a dedication and discipline to stop, meditate, ask, and wait. I had to make a shift from working in my head to listening with my heart, to split wide open and ask to be guided and open to receive. It has been necessary to embrace the silence and the way communication with Chloe has changed.

Early on in the woods, she asked me to learn her language. I am beginning to discern when the thought or feeling is her. I am becoming clearer on dream visitations and the messages they bring. It is a little like immersing yourself in a new culture. It takes effort and desire. I had to decide if I wanted to be content with my memories and the assurance that I would see her again . . . someday, or if I wanted to be with her now.

MUSIC
Music was a light and a curse. For months, I couldn't listen to it or sing. It touched me too deeply and stirred up everything inside me. There was

no genre that I could listen to. Some songs reminded me of Chloe; others touched my heart too deeply. I even stayed away from upbeat, funky songs, as they seemed to want to pull me to a happy place that was now foreign to me. I walked in silence without music. When I started dancing again, music came back into my life. Somehow, because my body was moving and I was focusing on technique, the pain that music often brought, didn't have a chance to work its way into my heart. Gradually, I could listen to music selectively, in short spurts. Still, after four years, it is making a slow entrance back into my life.

CHLOE'S IPOD AND ENYA

One night, I was charging Chloe's iPod. I turned it over and saw her name inscribed on the back: a gift we gave her one Christmas. I knew I couldn't listen to it with all her playlists. Music had become an emotional landmine for me. Still, I knew it would soothe in time, and I wanted to get it ready. I scrolled through her songs and found one by Enya: "How Can I Keep from Singing?" When Chloe was about ten, we did a dance to that song. The lyrics are meaningful to me more now than before. There are times when I find I can have a song in the midst of the storm. Other times, I can't. There is a phrase in this song that I cling to:

> *No storm can shake my inmost calm,*
> *while to that rock I'm clinging.*
> *Since love is lord of heaven and earth*
> *how can I keep from singing?*

CHLOE'S SONG

Chloe left us a gift in the form of a number of songs she had written and recorded which we had not heard before. Herm took these songs to a studio and recorded himself singing with her. At first, I could not listen to them and asked Herm not to sing them around me. In time, I read the lyrics and found comfort. Although I thought I would collapse when I heard the first song, I did not. The name of the song was "It's Alright" and I found a soft comfort in it.

One day I woke up hearing Chloe sing her song, "It's Alright." It was as if she was singing to me in the night to soothe me. I have wondered, as Chloe was writing these, if it was actually her soul or spirit writing, to leave this gift of comfort for us. Now I often hear these lines ringing in my head:

Well it's alright, everything's fine, just fine
so close your eyes, turn out the light.
It's alright, the sun might not be out tonight
but look to the sky, the stars are just as
bright.

If I sang you a song, would you sing along,
our words would follow everywhere we go
and give us the strength to overcome
what's in our way, and not let go till the
struggle leads us home.

Because Chloe was musical, much of the comfort she brings has been in song form. It has not been unusual to have a song play or appear at the exact point of need. This was especially true on the morning I drove into the parking lot at work, not at all ready to start my day. It had been a stormy, tearful drive down the canyon. I parked the car and collapsed into tears. I had been needing to know that Chloe was around—I decided to sit in my car and try to breathe and find some kind of centered place. But peace eluded me. I reached for the radio buttons. I have them programmed to my favorite stations, although I seldom listen to them.

A song I had never heard came on a station I never listen to: "I'll See You Again" by Celine Dion:

I will see you again
This is not where it ends
I'll carry you with me
Till I see you again.

Every piece of this experience has somehow propelled me into some type of research to make meaning out of what I felt. I needed to understand grief at every level and questioned whether healing was even possible. Could the unbelievable actually be believable? What was happening to my body and my brain?

The Brain

When I began working with Dillon on geometry in his junior year in high school, it took a lot of brainpower for me to get it all and stay with it. I realized my brain was doing something different. I noticed that I was not as emotional and felt a little steadier at times. I wanted to know more about the brain. I would have never thought that something like delving into math could help me in the midst of my grief—could it be that flexing the muscle of my analytical mind restored a greater balance of equilibrium to my thoughts? That brain activity actually plays a part in healing? If that were true, then perhaps I could choose particular activities to reset my brain.

When something traumatic happens, the left side of the brain is temporarily out of commission. This is the side that usually helps us make sense of events in an orderly, organized manner. This is the side that lets us know what is in the past, what is going on now, and what is in the future. It is also the side we rely on for solving problems. With this side of the brain temporarily out of the action, the right side of the brain stores the memory. One problem with that is that, to the right side of the brain, all time is here and now. That can cause a lot of problems when it comes to feeling as if a trauma that happened 15 or 50 years ago continues to be experienced in the brain as though it is going on now. That is why time does not heal all wounds.

The right side of the brain stores traumatic memories in bits and pieces instead of storing it in the logical, linear way the left brain does. All of the sights, sounds, smells, tastes, and stimulus information are stored without the story. Unfortunately, this can set up even non-threatening stimuli associated with the trauma like so many land-mines waiting to go off when the stimulus is encountered in the future.

Exploring information on how the brain reacts to grief helped me in a couple of ways. In the early days of loss, I could only process bits and pieces of information. If I received an e-mail asking me to respond to more than one or two questions, I quickly bypassed it, procrastinated, or just deleted it. I could have an entire conversation with someone only to come away from it realizing I had heard nothing. At work, I had to plan more carefully so as not to have to make sudden decisions. The process of decision-making was monumentally difficult. Brainpower was just generally not there. I removed myself from committee work and extracurricular activities so I could apply my brainpower to self-care.

I now understood why I was having irrational fears and even panic attacks. My right brain was saying that if it was a Sunday afternoon and I was home alone with Dillon, then tragedy was going to strike. There was no separating an event from the past and placing it in the present. Where was my left, logical brain when I needed it? This is why anniversaries of the event produced not just sadness but anxiety. My right brain was telling me that what had happened in 2010 was going to repeat itself in 2011 as well as in all subsequent years. It is why, on the way home from work one day, I went into a panic. I got home and burst through the door as a tearful train wreck, sobbing that Chloe wasn't OK. It was a tug of war. I knew everything was fine, but that other part of me was saying that what had happened in the past was happening right now.

When I started to see that reactions could form habits of fear, whenever a trigger appeared, I could say to myself, "This is 2012, not 2010." I could also choose a left-brain activity to help me reset my brain or to switch over to another channel. However, it took more than mantras and awareness. It took help from Chloe. The night that I had the train-wreck, sobbing attack was when I had the dream about the magnificent bird in the sky, and the next day was when I received the message about Chloe's constant presence with me on that ride up Caribou Road. This is yet another way in which both Science and Spirit have helped me in my grief.

CHAPTER 9

Suspending Doubt

The most beautiful and profound emotion we can experience is the
sensation of the mystical. It is the power of all true science. He to whom
this emotion is a stranger, who can no longer wonder and stand rapt
in awe, is as good as dead. To know what is impenetrable to us really
exists, manifesting itself as the highest wisdom and the most radiant
beauty, which our dull faculties can comprehend only in their primitive
forms—this knowledge, this feeling, is at the center of all true religions.

—ALBERT EINSTEIN

IN THE BEGINNING, I KNEW that the most helpful quest for me in losing Chloe
was to find her, and yet, that seemed impossible. I knew she was physically
gone. I was pushing the edge to even entertain that thought. Wasn't death
black and white? Still, something deep inside me knew I could find her, that
she was there, somewhere. So I just got quiet and asked. But there was that
part of me where my science brain took over, coupled with messages I heard
from the past, my culture, my church, and family that said, "You can't know;
you can only wait." And so I doubted. After every occurrence of hearing or
meeting Chloe, I was skeptical. I searched for all the reasons it could only be
a coincidence or my own distorted perception. As I was sitting with my sister
one day, she said, "You ask to find Chloe, and when she appears, you doubt."

From that day forward, I took a leap into believing. I suspended my disbelief and took the risk to believe and find even more.

Still, I was hesitant to approach this discovery of Chloe's appearance with others. Would I be met with disbelief, fear, sympathy? I didn't know how to initiate those conversations. Even if I did describe each event, it is only the tip of the iceberg as far as seeing or understanding what I actually experienced and knew and felt. The images conjured in an onlooker's or reader's mind might appear quite different than what I saw or experienced in all of its nuance and detail. Along with the actual event or message and image, there was a feeling that came to me in those moments. It was my intuition and a deep "knowing." In other words, you just had to be there.

I began thinking about the intersection of Spirit and Science. One day, I was meditating and talking to Chloe, asking her for guidance. I asked her if she could just bring me a message as I went through my day, as I had a lot to do and didn't have much time to meditate. That probably defeated the point of meditation, and I doubted that my request would yield any results as I perhaps hadn't followed the correct meditation protocol, but I had to feed the horses and get Dillon to the doctor, and I was up against time.

As I was driving to the doctor's office, some unexpected ideas started interrupting my thoughts and my music: *How do we get information in our world?* And then, *Information comes to us in different ways.* I started making a mental list of the ways we receive information while sitting in the waiting room at the doctor's office:

- Science is based on facts, observations, research, experiments, and intellect.
- Metaphysics or Spirit comes to us in messages sent directly to our intellect and heart. It can be conveyed through intuition, dreams, visions, events, images, senses, feelings, or experiences out of body.
- Physical messages are received through our bodies; waves traveling in and throughout. They are what we feel and sense; they are physical intelligence. A tightened muscle can be a message that fear or anxiety

is present. A tight or nauseated stomach can be a clue to reflect on what just happened or is happening in your life.

I felt a presence urging me to stay with these thoughts. Thinking about information in this way was somewhat new to me and I wanted to know more. The message continued: If we attach to only one means of gaining information, we are living in a limited dimension and acquire only limited information about ourselves, our lives, and our world. We cut off dimensions.

If we believe only in Science, we cut away information that could be gained from Spiritual dimensions. If we live only in the Spiritual dimension, we are cut off from a wealth of knowledge and information that Science offers us.

To be fully knowledgeable and gain complete information and messages, we must create an intersection of science, spirit, and the physical realms. For example, if you adhere to only that which can be proven, you will receive a great wealth of knowledge about yourself and your world, but you will only see it in part. You cut off your spirit and miss the information waiting for you there. If you are skeptical about Science because you believe it may diminish your spirit or your experience with God, you only see God in part and reduce your view of the complete picture. I am a skeptic on all sides. When I have a mystical experience, I ask myself if it was real, because I can't really prove it. Then I set out to disprove it, only to find out that I can't, which cycles me back around to my spirit.

Science can be baffling as well. What is proven in one generation may be altered or disproved in another. Take the science of nutrition. While it is supposedly based on research, intellect, and hard evidence, it has a way of giving us new messages as more is learned and technological advances are made. Fair enough. Mysticism has also made advances. What was once a mystery can now be known, if we want to know.

As I was pondering the relationship between Science and Spirit, I became curious about the great scientists throughout history. As they made their discoveries, were they met with mystical experiences that they could not explain or prove? Physics is a study of those phenomena that can be observed, measured and verified. Metaphysics is anything beyond that realm. I was surprised to find how many of them discovered something beyond the tangible. The British physicist Oliver Lodge, became a mystic and spiritualist after the death of his son. Lodge's work on electromagnetic radiation convinced him that an all-pervading "ether" filled the entire universe and linked everything together, effectively eliminating even the gap between life and death. It should therefore be possible, he reasoned, for a living father to communicate with his dead son.

Both Science and Spirit describe a force and energy that connects everything. We have separated religion and science into heart and head, when, in reality, one cannot exist without the other. Weighing and measuring alone offer a narrow perception of what exists in and around us. While Science has opened doors never before imagined, it is, still, one-dimensional and does not have the ability to explain everything. It is Science that helps me understand the physical aspect of death. It gives me the reality of that last breath and the absent footprint. It is the dimension in which my own physical being splits wide open and bleeds from the loss of Chloe. There is nothing to deny. Science has proven the loss. But it is the spiritual, metaphysical, stepping into the once unknown universe that has expanded my experience of living. It is a little like Alice in Wonderland falling down the rabbit hole, never knowing there was any more to experience than what already existed. What have I missed because of the notion that what is real is only what I can see, hear and touch? It's somewhat like walking past the gate to a lush, magical garden for years, but never entering. Then one day you are somehow compelled to enter and are breathless because you are in awe when you see what has been there all along. That is how I felt when I entered Chloe's world.

DREAMS

Dreams are not new to me. I have had a very active dream world throughout my life and remember dreams quite vividly. It has often been clear when a dream is a reflection of my waking life and emotional state, such as fear or anticipation of event, but I was not prepared for dreams in which Chloe was largely present. It was an amazing, comforting connection. There was a difference in the way Chloe appeared in dreams. While most images in my dreams were "dream-like", Chloe was as real as she had ever been. I could see her and feel her in full detail. Still, I was curious and wanted to know more. What I learned is that dream theories do not all fall into one basket, but various dreams serve different purposes.

Freud describes dreams as "wish fulfillment." Carl Jung suggested that dreams reveal both the personal and collective unconscious and believed that dreams serve to compensate for parts of the psyche that are underdeveloped in waking life. Calvin Hall takes a different focus in his belief that the ultimate goal of interpretation is not to understand the dream but the dreamer. G. William Domhoff has found that dreams reflect the thoughts and concerns of a dreamer's waking life.

I have found all of these theories and ideas to be true when I apply them to my own dreams. But none of them accounted for my experiences in my dreams with Chloe. Although these dreams certainly were about wish fulfillment, they went beyond that. There was something deeper, clearer happening. Connection with Chloe and a message for my life almost always presented itself. Something was different about these dreams, compared to my other dreams. There was an added dimension, a deeper sense. Instead of merely seeing events and colors, I was connecting to the events at a different level of feeling and seeing. Should I just dismiss them and dismiss myself as a crazy, grieving mother who needed to concoct such images and create my own new reality with Chloe? Although the dreams were comforting, and for that moment in time, I was with Chloe, they were also message dreams. At first I could only observe and be happy to see her again. But then, as I went deeper into them, I felt Chloe urging me, pursuing me to work with the dreams at a deeper level. She was my teacher. I had to close my eyes and not think about the images as much as just the feelings that were coming through. Then the images would start clicking into those feelings, and the message became clear.

Dr. Anne Reith, founder of the Impart Wisdom & Wellness Center, studies dream visitations. She describes these dreams as being "real" and vivid. A dream visitation will be remembered for days, months and years. The person will almost always appear in the dream to be completely healthy and loving. They will *rarely* appear sick or injured. They will *never* be angry, disappointed or depressed. They come with a purpose, to let you know that they are fine and that they want you to be happy. As I read her characteristics of visitation dreams, the words popped off the page, as they described exactly what I was experiencing when Chloe came to me in a dream.

Learning about dreams was intriguing, but I also realized that it didn't really matter what the physicists, neuroscientists, psychologists, theologians or metaphysicists had to say on the subject. It was my deep sense of knowing and experience that I could not deny. I knew what was happening, and I had to deeply trust myself and my intuition, and I had to trust Chloe. My sharing of these experiences is in no way an attempt to convince anyone of a particular position on dream interpretation. It is simply my experience.

When I began to ask Chloe questions that I needed answers for, I didn't specify how I wanted to receive them, but many of her responses came through dream visitations.

To be clear, I didn't get the message in the dream itself. It was only after waking and getting that nudge to put it together did I understand it. I felt Chloe teaching me how to find the message that she was trying to bring. For some dreams, it was not until several years later that I reread a dream account and then understood its meaning. At times, there was no message, but just a moment of connection and love. Some of them made me incredibly happy, but could result in sadness in the following days because of the reality of her absence here in the physical world. At the same time, they brought significant healing and continued connection.

When I realized that dreams were going to become a regular form of communication and connection, I started writing them down. There have been too many to recount in one chapter of a book and sometimes hard to relay the significance. The following are a few dream visitations that have held the most meaning for me.

Show Me Where You Are

A month after Chloe died, our family decided to get away for the weekend. It was Thanksgiving, and none of us were feeling quite social. It was the first time we had been on a family trip without Chloe. We entered the condo. It was a perfect space for us, and we all felt happy, but then the realization that we were only four instead of five left me feeling hollowed out. We moved in and out of laughter and tears, peace and vacancy, darkness and light.

At the suggestion of a friend, when I lay down to sleep, I asked Chloe a question. I said, "Chloe, show me where you are tonight. What is this place that you have gone to?" I thought that if I saw anything, it would be something new that I had never seen before, like a piece of heaven. I felt relaxed and drifted off to sleep. When I woke in the morning, I suddenly remembered the dream.

Chloe wasn't off in this "other world" place. She was standing right in the kitchen of the condo with us. She was going back and forth from her human form to her spirit form. Then she picked up a deck of cards and said, "Let's go play." At the time, I was just comforted to see that she was right there with us, and I could see her so clearly. I wasn't yet ready to embrace her spirit form, but felt her love.

Four years later, a new message from that dream came to me. Whether we are in spirit form or physical form, we stay connected. We just have to be willing to meet each other in our own spaces. The connection transcends the form. Chloe's answer to my request—"show me where you are"—was *"I'm right here."*

Questions for Chloe

The following three dreams came after asking questions that I needed answers to. They were also the most significant visitations I have had. These dreams I remember in the most vivid detail, every image, every feeling, action and even fragrance. They occurred near the beginning of her leaving, when I had no idea it was even possible to see Chloe again in this way. But one day, while sitting in the woods, I said to Chloe, "I want answers." I wasn't at all convinced that this was appropriate or even within the parameters of approaching someone in the spirit world. Was I being bossy? What were the rules? Still, I had try, I had to pursue answers to know about my daughter's new place. I asked three questions and got answers in three different dreams.

Question 1: What happened when you died? What was it like when you crossed over? How did you feel?

THE STADIUM DREAM

Our family was going to a sporting event. Herm left with Hope, and I came behind them with Dillon, who was a baby or young child. As I was trying to get to our seats, I had to go through a dark room. I could see the bright lights of the stadium on the other side, but I didn't like the dark room. I turned on the light, but the security guard told me it had to stay off.

I got into the stadium. Dillon was kind of sick, so I wanted to find a bathroom, but I wanted to find our seats first. When I got to our seats, I saw that they were at the top of the stadium. Chloe started walking down the steps toward me. She had a bright, cheerful, bouncy yellow dress on. It was gathered at the waist and then poofed out. I told her I needed to find a bathroom. She did too. She was happy and lighthearted. I noticed she had a wound behind her neck and three wounds on the back of her right leg.

Then we went to find the bathroom. I couldn't find one anywhere I looked. Then Chloe said she thought the only bathroom was way downstairs. I said that couldn't be, because it was dark down there. She said she was going down there, and I said I would keep looking, feeling nervous about the darkness. No matter which way I turned or which door I opened, no bathroom. Soon, Chloe came up from the dark place. She had not been afraid to go down into that dark room. She went back up to our seats while I kept looking. Finally, I got into the Yukon and went driving around. It was a busy city with people everywhere. I felt lost. Everywhere I turned was the wrong way.

This dream was full of dark and light. The stadium was amazingly bright and happy. Then Chloe went to a dark place, but wasn't scared. She came up into the light, and went to be with us. During this time, she saw that I was very lost and Dillon was not well. Her message, in answer to the question was: *"I went through a dark place, then came up into the light and I was with you."*

Question 2: How did you feel when you crossed over?

The Magnificent

I stated what I wanted to know before I lay down. I fell asleep. This is the dream I had:

We were at a barbecue event with people, food and music. It was small but festive, like a county fair. I was walking with Hope and Chloe. We were happy, and the mood was light. Chloe was so much herself. She was so real. I knew that she had died, but could still be with us. All of sudden, she started jumping up and down and getting excited. She said, "Mommy, look! There's the Magnificent." The best way I know to describe it is that it was like a music group on a stage, where the song and the instruments move you deeply. She was so excited and started running toward it. It was just like Chloe.

I knew she was leaving and I called to her and said, "Chloe, how will we communicate?"

She turned and responded, "In our hearts." I knew at that point that it didn't matter if we were talking in words, that the real communication was really in our thoughts and spirits. Then Chloe disappeared. I suddenly knew how to communicate with her. I wanted to find her, to go out to the field and just sit with her, but she was gone. I started crying. My doctor was checking me out and asking me all kinds of questions. I went out to the field. It was night. I put my coat down and lay on it and looked up into the sky. There were stars but also a rainbow going across the night sky. There was also a wispy cloud.

Chloe had seen something magnificent; she was excited and tried to tell me about it. She walked toward it. She gave me a message about how to communicate with Her. She was happy and lighthearted. During the time of her exuberant transition, I was in need of healers, but initially I didn't want them, or anyone, around me. All I wanted was to be alone with Chloe.

I don't know exactly who met her, who the Magnificent was. I do know that she absolutely wanted to go there. I can still feel that moment of absolute bliss in her, I feel it as I see the dream again in my mind.

Question 3: What is it like where you are?

The Plantation Dream

Last night, I had a dream of a beautiful plantation. There was a big, white house called the Main House. It was like a southern mansion and had some gold or brown parts on the columns. There was also another house off to the side in the trees. It was pure white and resembled a farmhouse. Across the grass from the farmhouse were two rows of joined cottages that people could stay in. The front row of cottages had a connected porch. Outside each cottage was a bed on the porch so you could sleep outside, under the stars. What impacted me most was, when I was by the plantation house, I looked up to see the hugest tree with pink blossoms spreading across the sky. The color and fragrance was mesmerizing. The grass was green and lush, and I could feel it under my feet. The climate was perfect, slightly cool and moist but not really humid, more refreshing. There were no insects and no threat of any type of wild animal. Everything was safe. I just stood there alone, feeling immersed in this wonderful place.

This was a "Chloe utopia." Surrounded by nature and a type of camping re-treat and luxury all in the same place. I don't think it means that this is what everyone will experience when they cross over. The closest thing that a human can imagine is something that engages every one of the senses at the same time. It's not even so much that "this is where Chloe is"; the greater picture is my recollection of how I *felt* being there. I now knew what she was experiencing in this place, a peaceful euphoria. Whenever I feel unglued or distraught,

I go to that place and breathe. I feel it, smell it, and see it all again and again. It is a healing place.

Chloe's Healing

When Chloe was 18, she began having stomach aches and digestive issues. We were experimenting with her diet and saw several doctors to try and resolve her illness. It was likely some type of colitis and we worked to help her feel better. I didn't ask her to show me how she had been healed through death, but I was grateful to receive this dream and message. It came on a night that our family was staying in a mountain condo on a weekend get-away.

Chloe was sitting in a hospital bed and I thought she was there because of her colitis. But she was sitting up, and she was happy, and we were talking. She had her hand on her stomach and said, "Mom, I feel so good!" In the meantime, Hope had phoned me and was having an appendicitis attack. I told Chloe I needed to go help Hope. She said, "OK, that's fine, but would you get me some ice cream first?" So I went and got her some ice cream and went to find Hope.

When I woke up, I wondered why Chloe would come to me as sick in a nursing home. The dream bothered me. Later, we rented bikes to take a trail ride. It was a beautiful ride, and I knew Chloe would have loved it, and I missed her. It was hard to accept the fact that she wasn't here. As we were riding I thought about the dream. I started asking her about it. I said I just didn't get why she would come to me in that way. Then I remembered that the message is rarely literal; you have to look deeper. The more I thought and asked her to help me with the message, the clearer it became. A hospital represents a place where people need help. Chloe wasn't there because she was sick. She was trying to tell me that her job now was to help people. If she had been there for her colitis, she would never have asked for ice cream. In the end, I got the message: *"I have people I need to help. I'm happy. I'm not sick. Go and help Hope; I have work to do."*

Once I worked through the message hidden in her visitation, I found I could relax, knowing that she was doing what she was meant to do and that I am here to help myself, my family, and others. We each had work to do.

I was in a happy, content place at that moment. I not only saw who Chloe was in the past, but I was seeing who she was now, in the present.

The Black Onyx Earring

I was somewhere outside—a farm, a fair, or something. I was handed a baby. It was new, warm, and only slightly moving. I felt awkward holding it, but it felt good. Out of the corner of my eye, I saw my favorite black onyx earrings lying on the ground. I kept looking at them, wondering how they got there and thinking that I should pick them up so I could put them back where they belonged. But as hard as I tried I just couldn't reach them. All the while I tried to get them back, I felt this small, warm life in my arms, laying against my heart, making subtle movements.

When I was driving home shortly after that dream, I was thinking about the earrings that I couldn't reach to put back in their place, and the baby I was holding with its subtle movements. At first I just said, "I don't have a clue what that means."

But I could hear Chloe say, "Work with it, Mom." I thought a little harder and deeper. Then I started to feel what had happened. The earrings were some of my favorites. They each had a solid, black stone encased in an ornate silver casing. After some work, this is what I learned: The earrings were dark, black. They represented death, a death that was out of place and couldn't be put back. Chloe's death seemed out of place, and I desperately wanted her back. But at the same time, while I kept looking over at those earrings and wanting to pick them up, I was holding a new life. It felt awkward but good. The baby's movements were the subtle movements of life returning. I heard the message, *"You don't have to take large steps. Just feel the movement of life."*

When we moved to Colorado from Virginia four years before Chloe's death, I left that one black onyx earring behind as it had no partner. Prior to losing it, I wore them almost every day so it wasn't surprising it showed up in a dream.

Four years after this dream, I was meditating and doing yoga in my Colorado home. A wave of grief came over me and I began to cry and ended up face down on the floor. I told Chloe how much I missed her and I needed to know if she was still around. I needed a tangible sign. I got through that time and went on with my day. The next morning, I woke up and stepped out of bed. Something drew my gaze to the floor and there, at my feet, was one black onyx earring. The one that had appeared in my dream. There had been nothing on the floor the night before. I know because I had been crawling around on the floor untangling computer cords. I had not seen that earring for over ten years. I reached down to pick it up. I froze in that spot, feeling a rush of disbelief and yet incredible love flow over me. I began to tremble, knowing how and why it had appeared. I put one foot in front of the other and inched my way to the living room to find Herm. I told him the story and asked if he thought I was crazy. He took my arm and led me to the table where I had completed a painting the night before. It was a portrait of a girl with a dragonfly whispering in her ear. The inscription I had added was, "Trust your heart."

RETURN

Last night, I had a dream that we were at some kind of church function. There was a lot of activity, food, music, and games. Chloe came in and went over to her friend Hannah. They hugged and sat and talked. They just stayed together, talking. I tried to participate in the activities, but kept dropping out. I felt glad that Chloe was there, but I also felt sad. I kept asking myself why I couldn't let it go. She was back now. It's like I knew something just wasn't right but I could see her so distinctly.

Then Chloe and Hannah went into a room. It was filled with yellow and orange light. Hannah had brought her gifts, a pink ring and a couple costumes including a fluffy tutu. There was so much brightness in the room. They commenced trying on the costumes. Their cheerful banter and joyful laughter could be heard from a distance. It was a jubilant reunion.

Then the event was over. I asked Chloe if she wanted to go on a family vacation or go home. She just wanted to come home. I said that she had been through a lot and probably just wanted to rest. In the middle of the dream, someone asked me how I was doing. I said, "You never get off of the train. You just redecorate it."

The train quote stayed with me for several days after the dream. Now, several years later as I reread it, I realize it's so true. I will never get to rewind my life to a place where Chloe was physically with me. But I do have to decide what I want the train to "look like" now. I've been working on some redecorating over the years. Although I'd like off the train at times, it is starting to reflect the new person that I am becoming and that is making me happy.

These are only a few dreams of many visitations from Chloe. She came mostly in the context of family and was always happy. Many times it was just a visit or a time of being close. Other times there were significant messages. When I woke up from each dream I always felt I had been with her and could still see and feel the events and our interactions in a very real way.

MESSAGES

"You don't have to work to earn intuition—It's only necessary to open your heart and listen to its quiet and subtle presence deep within."

—SONIA CHOQUETTE

I've decided I'm done with disbelief. Just because I have never experienced something in the past doesn't mean it isn't real or doesn't exist. So if there is any chance, even a very scant chance that it is Chloe, then that is what I will believe. It's not that I want to turn everything into a sign. I just want to stop being a skeptic. Chloe said our relationship would continue, and I have to believe that this is what is happening.

People ask me how I know it's her. What do I hear? As I mentioned earlier, hearing requires learning a new language and also believing. Way more is given to us every day than we are receiving, because we haven't tuned in. We miss so much of what is being communicated to us. Divine beings are always around us, trying to give us messages, but we are so often unaware. Their language is subtle and often quick. We have to meet them where they are. It is difficult to hear what's coming through with a cluttered mind or life. I have had to do a lot of clearing out of my mind and my physical space, sitting with more silence. Sometimes it is timing, or the message follows a direct question; other times, it is an impression or an idea that I hear that I know is not my own. More assistance comes from our spiritual helpers than we actually recognize.

As I became more emotionally and spiritually centered, and my awareness increased, I began receiving and recognizing more messages. I also learned that the nature of the message and the method of its sending differs for each individual. For instance, while eating lunch with some friends who had lost their son several months before Chloe, I was amazed at what they had experienced. They had received several texts from their son, something I had heard about but not experienced. The texts were short without much detail. It is not uncommon for spirits to communicate through electronics, but it wasn't one of the predominant ways I heard from Chloe. Our communication fell into a few categories; dream visitations were the most frequent and strongest; telepathy—receiving a thought or idea from her; objects appearing, as well as symbols, music and, at times, animals. They all increased as I tuned in more closely to the earthly and spiritual plane. This wasn't an endeavor I really ever planned on or had an interest in, but I have found myself here, feeling like I have been asleep for a very long time and am now waking up.

The following journal entries are messages or contact that came at different times and in various ways. Telepathy, the communication of thoughts or ideas by means other than the known senses, was the form of communication that I sometimes found the most challenging. Learning to differentiate my thoughts from Chloe's voice took careful discernment. At times I would ask for more clarity or a confirmation that what I was hearing was from her. Confirmations came in the form of a word appearing on a notepad, a song, an unexpected email or conversation with a friend. As I noted earlier, Chloe's voice brought a certain type of feeling, as an idea or thought that was the opposite of what I thought or believed, or it came after I had asked.

Apart from dreams and telepathy, objects appearing in unexpected places, were the most amazing gifts, bringing an affirmation that she really was around. They were also the ones that made me work the hardest to release my disbelief. Initially, I would ask family members if they had placed a certain item where it had appeared, discovering that not only had they not been moving these objects, but they often laughed when I asked if they had. I have learned that different spirits have different gifts and abilities and sometimes it takes practice and work to develop a certain skill. I don't know if Chloe was responsible for these alone or if she had a posse working with her. I do believe they were her intent and idea.

The following messages from Chloe are arranged into four categories; Appearing Objects, Twenty-One, Animals and Flowers and Appearing in Laughter. I observed Chloe with her dog Oscar several times and butterflies always seemed to bring a message or alert me to her presence. It took me a while to catch on to the humor piece but it makes perfect sense. Chloe had her own sense of humor and playfulness. It became clear that she had the desire to have fun with her family or at least to see us happy. Not all episodes of laughter indicated that it was Chloe. Timing and appearing at strategic times as well as an intuition that it was her helped me to recognize it as something she had orchestrated.

APPEARING OBJECTS

HEARTS

This morning when I woke up at 5:00 a.m., I felt shaky. I wanted to just crawl in a hole and cry, but the tears wouldn't come. I got up and started getting ready for work. I went to my dresser to get my earrings. Lying there was a heart pin that the kids gave me a long time ago. I don't wear pins, but the special ones that have some meaning I keep in a box with another box sitting on top of it.

I can't remember the last time I opened it—ages ago. The heart pin had been in that box on the bottom, but now it was sitting on my dresser. I wracked my brain to figure out how it got there. I can only think (although it is hard to believe) that Chloe wanted to say, "I love you"—something I really needed. I sat on my bed and cried. I pinned the heart to the bottom of my sleeve to remind myself that she loved me and I loved her.

I went through my workday feeling a sense of peace, being comforted by the heart on my sleeve. Before lunch, I stopped into the bathroom to wash my hands. All the bathrooms in our school have soap dispensers. Never have I seen a bar of soap anywhere; they certainly aren't part of the budget. I turned on the water and started to move my hands under the dispenser when I looked down to see a pink heart soap lying on the sink. I stopped, took a breath, and said, "Thank you."

STARS

When I went to bed, I turned off my light and noticed a glow-in-the-dark star on my nightstand. Although we had something like it when the kids were little, I had not seen any of them for years. When we moved from Virginia to Colorado, I had purged our belongings and a glow-in-the-dark star would not be likely to have made the trip. Still, it could have been tucked away in the bottom of one of the boxes. But the mystery still remained. I wondered how it got there because I knew I had not put it there. I thought about it from every angle, but I couldn't come up with any scenario that would have put that star on my nightstand.

The next day in school, I walked by a little boy, and he was drawing a star. A teacher came in after school and gave a prize to one of my students: it was her "star" award. A little girl had her sandwich cut in the shape of a star. When I went to riding lessons, there was a star sculpture on the wall of the bathroom that I had not noticed before. At night, Dillon came home and said that while he was waiting for Dad in the car, he saw a shooting star.

Later, I asked Hope and Dillon if they had put the glow-in-the-dark star on my nightstand, and they just laughed. There had to be an explanation, but I couldn't find one.

I thought a lot about what Chloe wanted to say through the star. The message that came to me is the five points of the star are to remind us that she is still a part of our family and we are all connected by light.

AMETHYST EARRINGS

Almost twenty years ago, I bought a pair of amethyst earrings for a job interview (I got the job). Several years later the girls started wearing them, and I ended up with only one of those earrings and hadn't seen the other for about four years. I was always hoping it would turn up because it was one of my favorites, so I kept the one I had. Today I was cleaning off my dresser and there were a few earrings lying there. One of them was the single amethyst earring. I picked it up and said, half joking, half curious, "Chloe, where is the other earring?" and I laid it back down. I had to stop working because I wanted to get to Dillon's football game. I was feeling pretty good and looking forward to a day of sunshine and outdoor activities. When I came back, I continued arranging my dresser. I picked up the amethyst earring and put it on one of the hooks of my earring stand, without really looking. Then I glanced back and realized that both earrings were there. I just stood there trying to find my breath. That's all I could do.

I had been talking to Chloe about my need to know where she is and for her to stay close. When I feel that, then it is easier for me to find some meaning in my own life and move forward. After finding the earrings, I felt Chloe's presence, like she was with me all day. Whenever I came across something of hers, I didn't get this immediate punch of sadness that says, "That was Chloe's." I just said, "That is Chloe's, but she doesn't need it anymore." She seemed to be so much in the present and not in the past.

BOUNCE DRYER SHEETS

When Chloe was a little girl, she loved Bounce dryer sheets. I had taken her to the laundromat a couple of times, and she always wanted that little box of Bounce dryer sheets from the machine. I always gave her money to buy them. She would smell them and touch them. She loved them even as she grew older. When we brought her things home from Alamosa after she died, there was a small box of Bounce dryer sheets among her items. She never lost her love for them.

At work, I was on the phone one day, and during the conversation, I was looking straight ahead to the top of a shelf that sits in front of my desk. It just didn't register what I was actually looking at. Toward the end of the call, I reached out and picked up a Bounce dryer sheet, neatly folded and clean. I suppose there may be some reason to use these in my 2nd Grade classroom, however, I did not keep dryer sheets at work. It didn't really dawn on me until I hung up the phone what I was holding in my hands. I knew it was Chloe's presence. I smelled it and put it on my face. I laid it on my computer. I want to keep it there.

Bounce dryer sheets have continued to appear in unusual places—under my bed, in a closet of photo albums, in a tub of camping gear, my car. I no longer say, "I wonder how that got here?" I just say, "Hi Chloe, thanks for showing up."

THE BIRTH BRACELET

One day I found Chloe's birth bracelet lying on my dresser, not in the enclosed box that I kept it in. I'm not sure how it got there. It was odd that it had found its way out of the box without my help. I just stared at it, at the date of her birth. A couple of days later, I noticed the bracelet was gone, although I had not moved it. I looked around but couldn't find it anywhere and went on with my day.

Later, I went upstairs to clean my room. I moved my furniture and cleaned everything. I was wondering if I might find the baby bracelet that had gone missing from my dresser. But it wasn't anywhere.

A month later, the day before Dillon's birthday, I decided to move the furniture in the living room and clean the floors. I pushed back the sofa and there, lying under it, was Chloe's birth bracelet. Somehow it had made it down from my upstairs bedroom and all the way under that sofa. I believe there was a reason it ended up there. Beside it lay a red, egg-shaped container of silly putty, neither of which had been there the last time I cleaned. Chloe had a love for silly putty and play dough, at every stage of her life. This experience also came on the heels of a dream I had the night before: Chloe had come for Dillon's birthday and wanted to decorate and make it special. I know she wanted give him something or be with him in some way. This was her gift and the bracelet let me know it was from her.

TWENTY-ONE

There are times when messages have come through themes, symbols, or ideas repeating themselves in different ways. The symbols don't seem out of the ordinary, but there's something in the way they are received or when and how I see them, in conjunction with a deep knowing, that leads me to believe they are messages. Numbers that I have come to recognize as Chloe's presence are the number twenty-one and her birth date.

Chloe played basketball on many teams. One of her recent numbers had been twenty-one, the jersey number Dillon chose after her death. While sitting at one of Dillon's basketball games, I was feeling Chloe somehow around me and yet missing her. I asked her where she was. At that moment, I looked up at the scoreboard, and one of the scores there had turned to the number twenty-one.

While Christmas shopping one day, I was missing Chloe and feeling her physical absence during the holidays. I felt myself going through the motions and hoping to get to the other side of the season. As we drove into the shopping plaza, I looked up and saw this on the side of a tall building: Forever XXI. I had never shopped there, and didn't even know a store with this name existed. This message was all about the timing. Twenty-one had come to symbolize her presence. She could have shown me her number in many different ways, but the word forever was on purpose.

ANIMALS AND FLOWERS

BUTTERFLIES

Butterflies have appeared for me at strategic times. They are always yellow, resembling a Swallowtail. I never ask for them, but if they are close to me I know it indicates a message or that Chloe is near.

I have been resisting the camper for over three years. It holds so much pain as it was one of Chloe's happy places, and we had shared many family times in it. It has become this looming darkness parked behind the horse arena.

Last summer, Hope wanted to sleep in it, so Herm popped it up in front of the house. I could not enter; I could not face it. And yet, I thought that maybe if I just went in and sat there and cried, I could get to the other side and the dark would turn to light.

About a month ago Chloe had come to me in a dream. The four of us were sitting outside the camper, but could not bring ourselves to camp because Chloe wasn't there. Suddenly she came marching past us and said, quite directly, "I don't care what you're going to do, but I'm going camping!"

The next day I went to feed the horses. As I was working outside, a yellow butterfly seemed to be playing with me and following me around. I finished my work and went up the steps to the house. I turned and faced the camper. The butterfly came up to me, swirled around, and then flitted down to the camper where it hovered and danced around. I felt that I was supposed to follow it, that Chloe was leading me to the camper to help me, but I chose not to go. I was afraid. My fear robbed me of that healing moment.

FLOWERS

One summer day, I was buying flowers. I came to a beautiful orange-and-yellow variety. They reminded me of Chloe, her favorite colors. I decided to get them and make a kind of "Chloe garden." I hoped the clerk wouldn't ask me too much, compelling me to tell my story. Chloe interrupted that thought immediately, saying, "Would you stop telling that story? It's not about death anymore. My story is about life! Focus on that." I stopped in my tracks. Although the process of grief should not be shortchanged or pushed away, there was some truth and even relief in that thought. I didn't tell the clerk about the orange flowers, and in some way, it took away my need to tell the story of death and led me to think about life, both mine and Chloe's. This was a pivotal message in helping me to refocus my thoughts and direction. The chipmunks ate all the flowers.

OSCAR

Today all I could do was stare out the window and gaze at Chloe's thriving plant on the window sill. Hope came and sat down by me and hugged me. I held her *hand. Herm and Hope left for basketball practice, and I just broke down and cried. Oscar, Chloe's collie-husky mix, came and put his paw on my leg, and I held it. I kept crying, and he just lay on the rug beside me. Then he came back to me and put his paw on me again. His eyes kept following something behind my back. He just kept looking back and forth. Then he went and checked in each room and came back to me. He seemed to see something that I could not. In watching him, he seems to sometimes sense Chloe's presence.*

One day, Herm and I were lying on the sofa talking about Chloe. Oscar came and put his nose under my hand. It made me sad, in that moment, to know that Chloe was no longer with him. We continued our conversation and I became un-aware of Oscar. All of a sudden, I looked across the room and Oscar was sitting on the blue sofa where he would often lay with Chloe. The only time he was actu-ally allowed on the furniture is when he was with Chloe. He wouldn't even think about trying it if Herm or I were in the room. He was an obedient dog. Now, we looked over at him in disbelief. First of all, we had not heard his loud, jingly col-lar as he leaped onto the sofa. Secondly, he was looking straight at us with a very peaceful look, not the usual shame if he had snuck onto the sofa while we were out of the room. Chloe must have either been sitting with him or her presence was somewhere in the room. It is the only way he would have known it was okay for him to be up there.

APPEARING IN LAUGHTER

Laughter is not unusual in our family and I am grateful that it has still found its place in our lives. It is very common for Hope and Dillon to engage in humorous banter lifting the darkest of clouds and pulling everyone into their hilarity. Most of the humor found in our interactions is not necessarily an indication of Chloe's presence. It is just pure fun. But again, Chloe's presence is all about timing and sometimes directly asking her to show up.

Mother's Day weekend was approaching and we decided to take our first camping trip without Chloe. The last time I had been in the camper was when Chloe was there. I only imagined pain upon entering it now. I decided if that is what was there for me then it was time to feel it. I swung the door open and stepped inside, but I felt nothing really and I was surprised by my reaction. On my way back from a trip to the bath house I asked Chloe if there was some way she could show up on this first camping trip without her. I didn't really know if, or how, that would happen but I had no expectations. The next day I found a Bounce dryer sheet among the dishes and knew that was her and I was comforted. Even though the weekend became a mix of tears and laughter, it was good to be camping again.

It was the end of the weekend, and we were preparing to leave. Everything was all packed up until we realized that Herm had locked his keys in the camper and there was only one way to get them: through the small access door from the storage compartment. We all looked at each other. There was only one person who could possibly fit through the space and was at least halfway willing to do it—Hope. She squeezed and contorted her legs into the opening until her torso was wedged partway in. The banter began. She began a commentary on the events, and Dillon was all too happy to chime in. Hope felt around and finally located the keys and managed to free her body from the compartment and climb out. Gut-wrenching laughter ensued. My experience with Chloe's ability to manipulate objects gave me a sense that she had orchestrated this event to make sure we didn't leave this weekend with sadness.

In the depths of grief, it is hard to imagine that there is any place to smile, let alone finding your way back into humor. This is one of the places that Chloe manifested her presence. It was quite unexpected, and it took a little while for me to understand what was happening. At certain times when I would ask her where she was, the question was almost immediately followed with a moment of hilarity.

FISHING

Another incident happened on a family fishing trip. No one in our family is even re-motely skilled at this sport, but we thought it would be fun. On this day, Dillon's idea of fishing was to stretch out in the reclining lawn chair and catch some sun while consum-ing as many snacks as he could. My own idea of fishing was a walk around the lake.

It was a peaceful, warm day. As I turned to return on the path, I stopped and looked out over the water. I missed Chloe, I told her it wasn't as good without her, although I was trying to be grateful for the sun and blue sky. I asked her where she was, if she was actually here with us today. I took a few steps down the path seeing Herm and Hope on the bank with their poles. Suddenly Herm cast his line out, and half of his fishing pole catapulted into the air, heading for the water. Hope immediately doubled over in a gut-busting roar at the sight of Herm standing there with half a pole. When he realized what he had done, he reared back in laughter. It was a priceless, hilarious picture.

BRIDGES TO HEAVEN: A GRIEF-HEALING WORKSHOP

In my continued effort to live well and healthy, I signed up for a grief workshop led by Sue Frederick, author of the book, Bridges to Heaven. *What made this attractive to me was that it wasn't solely focused on grief, but on how your pain can fuel your future. I felt like this life challenge that I had been presented with also brought some kind of change in my purpose. This particular grief workshop, held at Shambhala Mountain Center, is not only shared with the attendees, but also with the loved ones the participants have lost. It only makes sense to include them in this process. I wasn't exactly sure why I was there or what I was going to take away from the weekend. I knew I needed affirmation about the messages I was getting from Chloe and about writing this book, but I just wanted to remain open to whatever was there for me.*

I arrived before the others and got settled into my tent, but I felt a growing apprehension that this was going to be painful, and I had the sudden urge to bolt. I was sure I could have a meaningful experience just having some quiet time in this beautiful mountain retreat center. But there was something prodding me on, encouraging me to move forward and attend the workshop.

It is the fourth year and I am getting better at telling my story without being afraid and emotional. Listening to others and seeing how we are walking this path together gave me strength. After I was done telling my story, Sue, an intuitive herself, told me that I have been able to heal because of what Chloe is teaching me and that she has helped me to develop my intuition. She said that Chloe now works "in tandem with me." This is the point where I shed a few tears, not because this idea was new to me, but because it is what I had been experiencing and needed the affirmation that I was where I was supposed to be.

In a two-minute reading the next day, Sue asked me how the book was coming. I had never talked to her about it, and yet I wasn't surprised. This too, was a message I had been looking for so I could proceed with my writing.

During one session we did an activity on Spirit Writing—to ask for a message and then start writing. We first began quietly meditating. I was a little doubtful but immediately began hearing something in the meditation that preceded the writing. Then it started happening so fast that I could barely read my own handwriting. I didn't stop to think about it; I just kept writing. It went like this:

Cindy: What is your message for me?
Chloe: Time to move our connection to the next level.
Cindy: What is the next level?
Chloe: Do you really want to know?
Cindy: Do I have a choice?
Chloe: No.
Cindy: Do you really want it to go to the next level? Don't you have things to do?
Chloe: We have work to do.
Cindy: So the connection isn't about deeper communication, it's about getting some work done?
Chloe: Yes.
Cindy: How?
Chloe: Level up.
Cindy: How? What is the next level? Is it work? Is it a state of mind or spirit?
Chloe: Play.
Cindy: What should I do moving forward with my life?
Chloe: Teach—shift your focus.

It felt a little random and somewhat surprising, but that is how messages often come, leaving me to sort it out or watch it unfold. The two themes I saw here were "Play," which was quite surprising and new, and "Teach," but in a different context than my 2nd Grade classroom.

The next session also began with meditation. It was a peaceful, quiet environment. I closed my eyes and prepared to still my mind, but not far into my attempt, I heard an irreverent, humorous Chloe start bantering. I kept trying to bring myself back to the state of meditation, but it wasn't going to happen. She just kept interjecting something to make me laugh. Finally, I gave up and said to myself, "Just be with her."

That evening during Restorative Yoga, the same thing started happening. Everything was quiet, calm and reflective, but on my yoga mat the dialogue again turned humorous. When the teacher asked us to focus on our third eyes, I immediately saw one of those eyeballs on a spring bouncing out of my third eye. I couldn't find a state of meditation. I began to worry that I was going to laugh out loud, disrupting the sacredness of this space. I was relieved when it was finally over and I had been able to keep a lid on the chatter. Playful humor was becoming a new connection, a place I seemed not to be able to find before. I felt Chloe giving me permission to laugh, even in the face of unspeakable loss. The next, and final day of the retreat, I felt Chloe's presence with me in such a strong and humorous way, as if she was following me around in an unrelenting style, laughing and bringing a playful strong, energy into my space. For the first time, ever, I had to say, "Ok, Chloe, that's enough.

CHAPTER 10

Conclusion

IT HAS BEEN FIVE YEARS since the day I thought my life had ended. This is the hardest work I have ever done. I suppose that if I could have just accepted Chloe's leaving as final and been content with memories, maybe it would have been easier. But that was not the path for me. I don't cry as frequently as I did but still find myself collapsing into the darkness of living without her from time to time. I feel more gentleness than anger. God has been redefined for me, and my spiritual practices happen more in nature, meditation, and silence. I feel more deeply connected to a divine presence, but let it come in whatever form it may present itself.

When death or tragedy strikes, there are two stories that immediately run side by side. The story on the physical plane is one of injustice, devastation, heartache, and excruciating pain. But at the same time, there is a spiritual story happening. In Chloe's story, I experienced all the devastation of losing her. But in the spirit story, Chloe is unafraid and in the light. She dances toward the magnificent with such elation. She asks that her death be approached with only love.

As pieces of my heart heal, I am better able to hear Chloe and my Spirit Tribe with more clarity. I no longer have to resist the urge to lie on the couch and stare out the window all day. I feel a surge of creativity returning and am getting ideas for art projects that express my journey. I am preparing to paint my dismal basement stairwell with bright and whimsical characters and turn it into a place where I can write positive messages that will greet me each day as I go to and from work. I am OK with crying at any moment, knowing that in the next moment I may laugh.

Gone From My Sight

I am standing upon the seashore. A ship, at my side,
spreads her white sails to the moving breeze and starts
for the blue ocean. She is an object of beauty and strength.
I stand and watch her until, at length, she hangs like a speck
of white cloud just where the sea and sky
come to mingle with each other.

Then, someone at my side says, "There, she is gone."

Gone where?

Gone from my sight. That is all. She is just as large in mast,
hull and spar as she was when she left my side.

Her diminished size is in me -- not in her.

And, just at the moment when someone says, "There, she is gone,"
there are other eyes watching her coming, and other voices
ready to take up the glad shout, "Here she comes!"

And that is dying...

—Henry Van Dyke

Chloe Elise Weaver

You will be forever loved and alive in our hearts.

Love is eternal; connection is forever

-cindy weaver

A Letter to Hope and Dillon

Dear Hope and Dillon,

Many things have been said about Chloe. They attest to her charac-ter and priorities in life. She was kind and loved her friends and family. She worked at life, to grow and make the world a better place. She was also full of fire, and only you two can fully understand that.

Although this book is primarily about me and about Chloe, she is only one of my children. It would be just as easy for me to fill the pages of a book about my love for both of you and the incredible people you have become. You have fierce courage and deep compassion. I never wanted you to be put in the position of having to fight your way through heart-ache, fear, anxiety and paralysis. But you did and you didn't give up. I know there were times when you had no strength and tears consumed you. But you got up, you moved forward…again and again.

You have so much to offer the world. You have everything you need to heal yourselves and to help others heal. Adventure is your birthright. Live fully with complete joy.

I am proud of you both beyond measure. My love will always be with you in this life and the next.

♡ *Mom*

About the Author

Cindy Weaver is a teacher who has worked in both public and private education for 20 years. She has a Master of Arts in *Information and Learning Technologies* and a passion for creating websites and working with digital images. Dancing has always found its way into her life and she is presently taking Ballet, Jazz and Tribal dance classes.

She enjoys many creative endeavors from colored pencil, watercolor and nature-creations to collage and Art Journaling. Drawing faces is what intrigues her most. She has found that writing in any form helps her move through life and stay close to her heart. Her family has been her greatest gift and one that propels her forward.

Her home is in the mountains of Colorado which she shares with her husband, a dog, a cat, two horses and two grown children that come and go in between their jobs and travels.

http://www.cindyweaver2017.com

Acknowledgments

As I NAVIGATED THE LAST five years, every family member, friend, co-worker and even acquaintance has been present in some way. From heart-felt words and tokens to holding my heart in silence because words have a way of failing us when we are broken. Thank you for extending even a momentary thought or prayer.

I offer my heartfelt thanks to Cheryl Breault for her gentle and unrelenting prodding to help me turn my journal into a book. You believed in this project when I felt lost and unwilling to give myself to the world. Thank you for honoring your intuition and helping me find my own.

To Annie Nichol, my editor at *kn literary arts*, I offer you my deepest gratitude. You led me through this project with your expertise and sensitivity to the subject matter. You encouraged me to always reflect on my words and be true to my own voice. At times I was in poetry class and other times in boot camp. You are a master at your craft.

To Herm, Hope and Dillon, thank you for allowing me to laugh and cry in my own time. Your love has carried me through impossible waters. Herm, thank you for helping me to see that writing this book could be "life-giving" when I was sure it would only bring pain.

Thank you, Chloe, for staying close and helping me see you as you truly are. For teaching me about a place I knew nothing about. You talked me down off the cliff many times and kept me moving forward. Your love is not a distant memory, but it lives and breathes in my life every day.

Made in the USA
Lexington, KY
13 August 2016